CITIES
IN THE MARCH OF
CIVILIZATION

INTERNATIONAL LIBRARY

BARBARA HABENSTREIT

CITIES IN THE MARCH OF CIVILIZATION

COLLINS · PUBLISHERS
London · Glasgow

FRANKLIN WATTS, INC.
New York

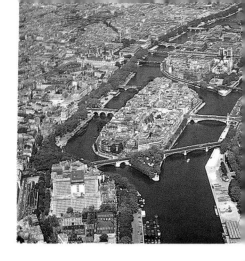

First Edition 1973

ISBN 0 00 100138 8 (*Collins*)
SBN 531 02114–9 (*Franklin Watts*)

CONTENTS

CHAPTER 1

THE

URBAN

OCTOPUS

The floating city juts up unexpectedly from the waters of the North Sea, twenty-five miles off the coast of England. Visitors approaching by boat can see nothing but the 180-foot-high (55 metres) circular wall that surrounds the metropolis. Outside the wall lies a ring of floating cushions that deflect the waves and create a "moat" of calm water, so that the city itself is protected from the churning seas.

The boat moves slowly through the single opening in the city wall and docks at a large harbour in the entry channel. As the passengers disembark, they see that the interior of the city resembles a huge amphitheatre, with apartment houses, shops, restaurants, theatres and power installations built on stepped terraces lining the inside of the wall. It is almost as if the 30,000 residents of Sea City were living on the broad ridges of a concrete and glass mountain that sloped gently down towards an enormous lagoon at the bottom.

Encircled by the terraced wall, the lagoon contains clusters of man-made floating islands that house offices, factories, government buildings, schools and other public facilities, as well as private homes and estates for some of the wealthier residents.

To explore the lagoon and its many islands, the visitors board electric-powered water-buses that can make round trips in just twenty-five minutes. Electricity is used instead of petroleum to avoid pollution of the lagoon, and when boats need a "refill" they can pull up to one of many battery-charging stations.

In Sea City, the petrol station is obsolete. So is the car. Transportation along the wall terraces—connecting apartment houses with stores, clubs and restaurants—is accomplished by escalators, travelators and covered walkways.

Just like many land-based cities, Sea City is a fairly self-sufficient community. The residents work in a variety of industries, the most important of which is the exploration of undersea natural gas. But there are also several fish canneries; a boat-building plant; factories that process seaweed into fertilizer; fish farms that cultivate oysters, clams, lobsters, trout, salmon and eels; and a desalination plant where salt water is turned into fresh. Most of this water is used by Sea City itself, but the surplus is exported to arid regions throughout the world.

Supplies are brought into the floating metropolis by barge, but residents travel to and from the mainland by helibus—a vehicle that takes off and lands like a helicopter,

Model of a floating city built by scientists at the University of Hawaii. Such a city could be constructed in the waters off the island of Oahu, to relieve population pressures.

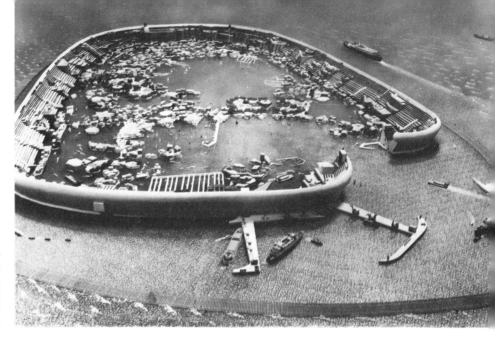

In Sea City—England's concept of the city of the future—residents would live in attractive flats built into the city's terraced wall.

but can also tuck in its rotors and fly like a normal aeroplane. The twenty-five-mile flight to the mainland takes fifteen minutes and costs about $1.00 or 40 pence.

There is no urgent need, however, for the residents to make frequent trips ashore, for Sea City provides them with almost all the services and amenities they could want. Most of them live in centrally heated, air-conditioned apartments on the terraced city wall. At their disposal are libraries, a 200-bed hospital, clinics, dental services, art galleries, cinemas, museums, churches, open-air tea gardens, and social centres. The central basin of the lagoon is reserved for swimming, sailing, water-skiing and skin-diving, while some of the wall terraces have been set aside for a football field, tennis courts, bowling greens and croquet lawns.

The marine city is small enough—4,700 feet (1,433 metres) long by 3,300 feet (1,006 metres) wide—for people not to have to travel very far either to work or to play. And despite the fact that the whole urban island was artificially built, its clean water, fresh air and beautiful lagoon make it seem more natural and unspoiled than the polluted, congested cities on the mainland.

Twenty-first century

Sea City may sound like a fantastic dream—perhaps as fantastic as it once seemed that men might someday walk on the moon. But just as modern technology has made moon walks possible, it has also made it possible to build whole cities that float in the ocean.

Sea City does exist, although only on the drawing-boards. It was designed by a team of Britain's leading architects and engineers and unveiled to the London public in February 1971. The floating city was depicted as the twenty-first century's answer to the need for more urban living space, and its creators left little doubt that this type of city would become a reality within the next few decades.

Floating cities are also being studied by Japan, where some of the most prominent urban planners are insisting that Tokyo should expand out into Tokyo Bay rather than swallowing up any more of the surrounding land. Scientists at the University of Hawaii are making similar studies, with the idea of building a floating city several miles off the island of Oahu.

These man-made floating cities may be one way of coping with the impending urban crisis, for throughout the world people are pouring into the major cities at an alarming rate. Urbanization is occurring more rapidly than ever before in the history of the world, and the earth's population as a whole is multiplying by great leaps. The United Nations has estimated that the current world population of about 4,000,000,000 may double in the next fifty years, with the bulk of this increase occurring in the already congested urban regions.

The results of such growth could be catastrophic, for many cities in Asia and Latin America are already swollen with surplus millions and have no more room to expand. Cities everywhere are in the grips of a housing shortage, and the problem is rapidly growing worse. New cities are urgently needed to house the world's bulging population and to provide jobs that are generated by urban-industrial growth. Yet the existing farmlands must also be preserved to feed the growing multitudes.

While city and country vie for precious space, 70 per cent of the earth's surface remains practically untouched—the 70 per cent that lies under water. This is why urban planners and architects are now exploring the oceans as a possible environment for tomorrow's cities.

The idea is not a new one, for many cities and countries have reached out into the sea to acquire more living space. The people of the Netherlands first began building dikes and pumping out sea water to expose more land about AD 1000 or earlier. Today, Dutch cities, farms and airports stand on this reclaimed

The former island of Urk (above) *was greatly enlarged and attached to the Dutch mainland (below) by means of empoldering—building dikes or levees to reclaim underwater land and make it suitable for agriculture.*

land that lies below sea-level.

Elsewhere, cities have expanded by means of land-filling—that is, by dumping earth into the shallow waters that lie beyond their shorelines. Another means of expansion has been to drive concrete or steel piles into the sea floor to support structures that tower above the water as if on stilts. Pilings can be

A two-storey building, located on a platform in the Gulf of Mexico, houses workers who are drilling for offshore oil. The helicopter on top of the building provides quick transportation to the mainland.

used several miles off the shore, and a number of petroleum companies have set up housing and work facilities on such pilings to aid in the hunt for offshore oil and gas.

One structure of this type—the Lema Platform in the Gulf of Mexico—is five storeys high and houses twenty-six men in air-conditioned, carpeted quarters, complete with colour television. The $800,000 (£300,000) structure contains a boat landing on the first deck and a heliport on top, gas-powered generators that provide electricity, a distillery that makes salt water potable, and its own sewage-treatment plant.

If such elaborate, self-sufficient structures are already in operation, it may not be long before entire man-made cities are protruding from the seas, helping to ease the population crush on the mainland.

The tentacles of the city are not only reaching towards the sea; they are stretching upwards as well. Skyscrapers are a familiar sight in many of the world's major cities, and it is now technically possible to build them as high as 150 storeys.

It has been estimated that all of Chicago's business area could be housed in twelve 150-storey towers, each with 3 million square feet (280,000 square metres) of rentable area. These superstructures could easily replace the 154 major office buildings that are now spread throughout the downtown area, leaving ample room for housing, parks and gardens in the heart of Chicago's business section.

The city already has some of the world's tallest buildings, including "Big John"—the 100-storey John Hancock Building that contains 705 residential apartments in addition to offices. With a population of about 12,000, "Big John" is practically a city in itself. When the building was nearing completion several years ago, the advertisements proclaimed:

Live Uptown . . . Work Downtown. You Can Commute by Elevator in Seconds.

People who live and work in the building—also known as "vertical city"—have hardly any reason for venturing outside it. The first 5 floors contain banks, stockbrokers' offices and retail shops. The next 7 floors have parking spaces for thousands of cars, followed by 28 floors of office space. The 44th floor serves as a "sky lobby", containing a drugstore, barber's shop and other small stores and services. Apartments begin on the 45th floor and go up to the 92nd. Above this are 8 floors containing restaurants, an observation deck and mechanical equipment.

But, as residents have found out, living in the stratosphere has certain disadvantages. A power failure that halts elevator service can imprison

People who live on the upper floors of the 100-storey John Hancock Building in Chicago have a panoramic view of several states from their apartment windows.

people in their vertical city or leave them stranded in the street. Although the views from the upper storeys are magnificent, residents cannot always tell what the weather is like because they are often above the level of the clouds. They have to make a trip downstairs to see if it is raining outside.

As large as it is, "Big John" is about to be dwarfed by the new Sears Building in Chicago that will rise 110 storeys and provide floor space equal to sixteen city blocks. At 1,450 feet (442 metres), the Sears building will be the world's tallest skyscraper, edging out New York City's 110-storey World Trade Center by just 100 feet (31 metres).

Despite the protests of critics who complain that the steel and glass giants are ugly and dehumanizing, more skyscrapers are springing up in every city where land is costly and scarce. It is hard to match the economic benefits of building upwards. The Sears building, for example, takes up just one acre (4,047 square metres) of ground space while providing offices for 16,500 persons. (Another two acres, however, are being used for a plaza surrounding the building.)

Skyscrapers have also invaded the major cities of Europe, Asia and Latin America, although not in large numbers as yet. Sometimes these new buildings have touched off angry battles between those who want to preserve the grace and harmony of the older architecture and those who claim that the new superstructures are necessary to cope with the swelling population and business boom. In London, controversy flared over the construction of a 36-storey tower on the southern edge of Hyde Park, drastically altering the neighbourhood. Similarly, many Parisians were furious about the complex of offices

The twin towers of the World Trade Center in New York City (not yet completed in this photograph) dominate the skyline of lower Manhattan. The 110-storey Trade Center displaced the Empire State Building as the world's tallest skyscraper.

and apartment buildings that went up over the tracks of the old Montparnasse railroad station. One of these buildings soared 60 storeys, creating the biggest change in the low Paris skyline since the construction of the Eiffel Tower in 1889.

On the outskirts of Paris, a whole "satellite city" of high-rise offices and apartments is now under construction. The complex—called the Quartier de la Défense—is intended to serve as a new urban centre that will lure many businesses and industries. Begun in 1958, the $1,000,000,000 (£400,000,000) project covers 2,000 acres (810 hectares) and is scheduled for completion in 1978. It will contain twenty-five office towers, apartments for 50,000 people, an exhibition hall, a shopping centre, theatres, restaurants and underground parking for 25,000 cars.

It is hoped that the new complex will relieve some of the congestion in central Paris, where traffic has become so heavy in rush hours that buses crawl along at five miles an hour—the same speed as horse-drawn carriages.

In an effort to deflect further commercial growth away from Paris

altogether, the French government is building eight new towns throughout the country as alternate growth sites. The French "new towns" concept is not unique. It was pioneered in Britain at the turn of the century, and now all of Europe is busily building new towns. The Soviet Union alone has constructed more than eight hundred since the Revolution of 1917.

Urban woes

As population pressures increase, urban problems multiply. At the start of the 1970s, cities everywhere were plagued with traffic and pollution problems, housing shortages, and other woes. A glance at the 1970 *New York Times Index*, for example, shows just how widespread the dilemma had become:

TOKYO, JAPAN—Tokyo banned traffic from four main downtown areas, including the Ginza, every Sunday to curb air pollution.

SANTIAGO, CHILE — Squatters' camps on the outskirts of Santiago were organized by the revolutionary Left. Some of the homeless forcibly occupied newly completed, scarce public housing.

ROME, ITALY—Romans spent

hours in congested traffic to reach nearby beaches, all of which had been declared unsafe because of pollution from raw sewage, poisonous industrial wastes, and other sources.

NEW YORK CITY, U.S.A.—The 1969 crime rate here was nearly twice as high as the national average for 1969.

NAPLES, ITALY—The city was plagued by faulty sewers and a rash of collapsing streets and houses, all due to uncontrolled building speculation fed by a population boom.

NAIROBI, KENYA—Shanty dwellers marched in front of the new $6 million (£2·5 million) Hilton Hotel to protest the burning of their homes during a slum clean-up drive.

LONDON, ENGLAND—A plan to encircle London with a massive superhighway system might be delayed until the end of the century since new estimates showed that the project would cost 40 per cent more than anticipated.

LIMA, PERU—Government gave some eighteen hundred squatters in slum area on Lima's outskirts title to land they had been occupying illegally.

MANILA, THE PHILIPPINES—The

Two nineteenth-century inventions—the passenger elevator and the steel construction skeleton—made the development of high-rise buildings possible. Today skyscrapers have become a familiar sight in cities the world over.
Top left: *Mexico City;*
top centre: *London;*
top right: *Tokyo;*
centre left: *Cairo;*
centre right: *Berlin;*
lower left: *Bucharest;*
lower right: *Tel Aviv.*

A blanket of polluted air envelops New York City.

Roman Catholic Church planned an $11 million (£4·5 million) resettlement project for poverty-stricken squatters in Manila. About eighteen-hundred slum dwellers were to be moved to a co-operative farming village in nearby Rizal Province.

SAIGON, SOUTH VIETNAM—Disabled veterans who could find no place to live in this city staged a protest by putting up their own shacks on public property. Meanwhile, other veterans demonstrated to prevent the destruction of their shanties in Saigon. As a result, the government cancelled plans to tear down 3,000 shacks.

NEW YORK CITY, U.S.A.— Thousands of air travellers were reported to be by-passing New York City because of harrowing traffic jams and overtaxed parking facilities at Kennedy International Airport.

ROME, ITALY—Strong vibrations from construction work on an urgently needed subway line endangered buildings along a five-mile stretch. Huge cracks appeared in walls, and residents lived in fear that the ceilings might collapse on their heads.

BUENOS AIRES, ARGENTINA—This city was in the midst of a crisis due to a severe housing shortage, steadily

rising unemployment, crime, and runaway inflation.

In country after country, the picture is very much the same. Too many people are pouring into the urban regions, and the cities are hard pressed to supply the necessary transportation, housing and other vital services.

Traffic is among the worst of the problems. The street patterns in the

This traffic tie-up on a German autobahn is just one example of the transportation problems that plague most major cities.

Houses are clustered tightly together in Tel Aviv, Israel's diplomatic capital and, with Jaffa, the largest city, with a population of about 400,000.

Indian cities are among the most congested in the world, yet peasants from India's impoverished rural areas continue to migrate to the urban centres.

heart of most European cities date back to the Middle Ages and are just not fit for motor traffic. A comparatively small number of cars and trucks can cause monumental tie-ups. In the lovely historic section of Amsterdam, with its charming canals and narrow cobblestone streets, pedestrians are as likely to be run over by a car on the side-walk as anywhere else. With little room to manoeuvre, motorists use the sidewalks for turning round and even for parking. In Rome, where many workers still go home for their midday meal, there are four horrendous rush hours to contend with each day instead of the usual two. Vienna, Florence and Rome are among the cities that have resorted to a ban on motor traffic in their older, central parts.

Wherever possible, Europeans have been busily changing their old street patterns to try to cope with modern traffic. Streets have been widened, plazas enlarged, traffic circles redesigned and urban express-ways built. There has also been heavy emphasis on expanding mass transportation facilities. Stockholm, Rotterdam, Helsinki, West Berlin, Munich, Hamburg, Prague, Buda-pest, Rome, Milan, Madrid, Barce-lona, Lisbon, London and Paris have all been building or extending their subway lines since the end of World War II.

Although cities in the past have been confronted with other prob-lems that may have been equally bad or worse, never before have so many millions of people been affected by urban difficulties. Until the nineteenth century, only a small fraction of the world's population lived in cities. The vast majority of people lived in rural areas, and their lives were untouched by either urban progress or urban problems. How-ever, the explosive growth of cities

This sleek modern train is part of the West Berlin subway system, which was recon-structed and expanded after World War II.

over the last one hundred and fifty years has affected all but the most isolated tribesmen and has drastic-ally altered the pattern of human existence. Mankind's present and future now depend largely on the fate of the cities.

At this point in history, when the urban influence is so pervasive, it is almost impossible to envision the world before there were any cities. Yet the whole urban phenomenon is relatively new. The oldest known cities date back only five or six thousand years, and archaeologists can now almost pinpoint how and where the first cities came into being.

CHAPTER 2

WORLD
WITHOUT CITIES

For thousands of years the hot desert wastelands that dominate much of the Middle East have stood barren and lonely. Only small, scattered villages break the monotony of the bleak desert landscapes, and Arab nomads roam from place to place in search of food for their goats and sheep. Life is harsh in these arid regions of Iraq, Jordan, Syria and neighbouring countries, where temperatures can climb to 130 °F. (54·4 °C.) and scorching desert winds blow sand into every crevice.

But it was not always this way, for these lands, now so inhospitable to human life, were among the first places where civilization began.

The seeds of this civilization are buried in huge mounds that tower above the flat desert terrain. Covered by the sands of centuries, these ancient mounds look like natural hills and ridges, but in fact they are mountains of rubble. They can be found in many parts of the Middle East, especially in Mesopotamia— the area around the Tigris and Euphrates rivers in the country of Iraq.

Over the centuries, many legends have been told about these mounds. Arab nomads and villagers believed they marked the sites of fabled golden cities of the ancient world. But it was not until the middle of the

nineteenth century that archaeologists first began poking into the giant heaps—and found that the legends were very nearly true. The desolate, sandy hills contained the debris of some of the world's oldest cities, a few of which were far more splendid than any built by modern man.

Excavations of these mounds— called "tells"—are still going on, and as archaeologists dig deeper down, they are gradually uncovering the history of ancient urban man.

The ruins of the ancient village of Tchoga Zambil, Iran, blend into the arid desert landscape that characterizes much of the Middle East.

Desert mounds called "tells" often contain the remains of ancient towns and cities. Archaeologists are digging out the remains of Nineveh from the Kouyunjik Mound in Iraq.

A nomadic existence

Of course, man's history goes back much further than the history of his cities. For nearly 600,000 years of human existence, there were no cities or even villages. People lived as nomads, roaming the earth in search of food and water. Like all other creatures, men had to hunt for their meals because they did not know how to produce food themselves. The natural yield of the land could support only about ten people per square mile on the average, so men had to travel in small, mobile groups, unhindered by many possessions. They spent their days searching for fruits and berries, poking in the ground for edible roots and catching small animals and fish. It was feast one day, famine the next, for they did not know how to save and preserve leftover food when the hunting was good. The constant struggle to find enough just to stay alive was the dominant activity of their world; they had little time or energy for other pursuits. If the food supply in one area ran low, they had to move on elsewhere to avoid starvation. It was impossible for them to settle in one spot since they had no control over nature.

Then—perhaps around 10,000 BC or earlier—men made the most vital discovery of all history. *They learned how to plant and grow their own food.* This discovery set men apart from the animals and it was the basis for all future civilization.

Among the earliest places where the discovery of agriculture took place was in the hilly regions of northern Mesopotamia, in what is now Iraq. This area was particularly well suited to a settled type of life. Various grains could be found growing there, and early forms of today's common food animals, such as cattle and pigs, roamed the hills and ridges. If it was not quite an earthly paradise, at least it was a place where people could camp for a while and enjoy a plentiful supply of food and water.

Some time after wandering into this hilly area, groups of semi-nomads made the crucial switch from gathering food to producing it. Exactly how this came about is unknown, but somehow they discovered the secret of growing enough of their own food to sustain themselves. Although they were undoubtedly not the first people in the world to accomplish this, they were among the most important in the cycle of history.

They learned how to plant wheat and other grains, as well as peas and beans. Soon they no longer had any thoughts about moving on. They had discovered a new way of life in which they did not have to wander about the earth. They could settle down where they were, cultivate the land and make a permanent home for themselves.

Psychologically this was a tremendous step. People do not easily abandon the only life-style they have ever known, and many of the early nomads probably continued their free-roaming ways with nothing but scorn for the nonconformists who had settled down.

But apparently the settlers had few regrets. Within a short time (which might have been about one thousand years), they were building fairly complex shelters for themselves out of mud bricks. These long, narrow homes were divided into several rooms.

The early settlers also domesticated many of the animals that they had found wandering about, and they became the world's first cattle breeders. They began as well to make tools to farm their crops and pound their grain.

By about 7000 BC, the Mesopotamian hill people were well on their way into the world of the future. While most of the earth's human population was still leading a nomadic existence, their farming settlements flourished. Over the next few thousand years, their descendants learned the art of making storage vessels and pottery, and of decorating them with exquisitely intricate designs. They built larger, fancier mud houses and became far more sophisticated in working the land.

Similar advances were taking place elsewhere, and as the various communities became aware of each other, they began engaging in trade. Surplus grain was swapped for semiprecious stones, ornamental shells, and paints, which were found in such—in those days—distant lands as the Turkey and Iran regions. Large herds of cattle, goats and sheep enriched the communities, and here and there people began paving the ground round their houses with cobble-stones, so that their little farming settlements took on the appearance of thriving villages. Copper and other metals came into use for making tools and jewellery, and gradually the Stone Age gave way to the age when metals were used.

But even though these north-

ern Mesopotamian villages were flourishing and prosperous, not everyone was content. Some people found the life there oppressive. Perhaps they were not as well off as their neighbours, or did not get along with them; or perhaps they were just restless and wanted to see what lay beyond their small villages.

Whatever the reason, sometime during the fifth millennium BC groups of the restless or discontented began migrating down from the hilly regions into southern Mesopotamia, bringing their knowledge of agriculture with them. Although

Sumerian seal, dating back to 3500 BC, shows men walking with a harnessed ox. Horses and dogs were among the other animals also domesticated by ancient man.

A statue called "A Ram in a Thicket," created out of gold, silver, shells and lapis lazuli, is an early example of exquisite art work created by combining a number of materials.

most of this land between the Tigris and Euphrates rivers was too dry for farming, there were extremely fertile regions along the high banks of the rivers.

The wanderers settled down here and began the task of cultivating the virgin soil. But they found that they had to change their farming methods because there was not enough rainfall for the crops to grow. Instead, the farmers had to rely on water from the rivers, which were in spate, sometimes to overflowing, during the spring months as a result of melting snow from the hills and mountains in the north. During flood periods, the normally arid valley between the Tigris and Euphrates was wholly or partly under water.

At first the new settlers—who were called Ubaidians—stayed very close to the high river banks and practised a simple, primitive type of agriculture. But gradually they learned that they could bring water to more land by channelling the flood waters into a series of canals that they built in the arid, low-lying river valley.

This type of agriculture, based on irrigation, was immensely successful, and it was not long before the people in the Mesopotamian valley were producing more food than they ever imagined possible—far more than they needed to feed themselves. The relatively small areas of fertile land could support large numbers of people, enabling the farming communities to become more densely populated.

Other groups of people began drifting into the region. In about 4000 BC a tribe of Semitic nomads settled down there. They were joined in about 3500 BC by the Sumerians, who probably came down from central Asia via Iran.

It was the Sumerians who were the driving force behind the world's first true urban civilization. Endowed with inventive minds and a restless curiosity, they intermingled with the other inhabitants in the Mesopotamian valley and infused the whole region with their dynamic culture. The Mesopotamian area became known as Sumer, for the Sumerian culture held sway here for the next fifteen hundred years.

With the Sumerians leading the way, the small farming villages that had sprouted along the Tigris and Euphrates began to make rapid advances. The sudden burst of progress was also due to the fact that for the first time anywhere, the people could count on a stable agricultural surplus.

If the discovery of agriculture was the first stage in the rise of cities, the production of a food surplus was the second. At last people did not have to apply most of their time and energies to securing enough to eat. The Mesopotamian valley, irrigated by its intricate system of canals, produced more than enough food for everyone. This meant that some people could gradually be released from farming chores, while the rest worked the land to feed the whole community.

Apparently the first people to drift away from agricultural work were the priests, who were now able to devote their full time to religious matters. The Sumerians were a religious people, and their villages were centred round large temples. Even the very earliest Ubaidian settlers had built temples at the same time that they built their homes. They believed that their gods needed places to live as much as they did.

The first temples were small and very plain, but as the villages prospered and the Sumerians came to dominate the region, the small temples were enlarged over and over

again. In time they became very elaborate structures that towered over all the houses, so that each village could be identified at a distance by its temple-tower. The villages expanded round the temples, which served the entire population and helped unify the people. Gradually the Sumerians transferred their loyalty from their family or clan to their temple-town.

All religious, social and intellectual activity centred in the temples, under the leadership of the priests. It was they who controlled the religious rites, composed hymns and prayers and performed sacred rituals. Later on, they also took on non-religious chores, such as administering the distribution of food —a process that became necessary as more people turned to non-farming occupations.

Surplus grain and other foodstuffs were stored in the temple warehouses so that the people could be sure of a food supply even during hard times. It was not long before temple accounts became so involved that priests were forced to devise ways of keeping records. Some of the earliest known examples of writing—script cuneiform impressed into clay tablets—were found in these Sumerian temples. This has led historians to believe that the priests were the first scribes. It was also in the temples that the people came together to talk, argue and exchange ideas, so that the temples were the centre of intellectual ferment.

Top: *a wall carving in an ancient Sumerian temple at al-Ubaid.*

Left: *reconstruction of the interior of the al-Ubaid Sumerian temple, with the wall carving in the background.*

Left: *Sumerian priests devised cuneiform writing as a means of keeping records. The Brick of Ur-Gur, dating back to 2500 BC, records the building of a temple in Erech.*

Bottom: *cuneiform script, one of the oldest forms of writing in the world, underwent so many changes over the millennia that the later cuneiform bears little resemblance to the earliest pictographs.*

As the villages grew larger and the amount of land under cultivation increased, the people faced new problems. Their complex agricultural system, dependent on irrigation canals and reservoirs, had to be managed by the community as a whole; it could not be left to individual farmers because it was all interconnecting. The canals had to be dug out, cleaned and repaired regularly. If a few sections were neglected, the whole system could get hopelessly clogged. Furthermore, there were arguments over boundary lines and water rights that set people at each other's throats.

The old collective methods of settling community disputes did not work when the community grew larger. The townspeople could not spend all their time thrashing out difficult problems; they had other work to do. Gradually, they began appointing a few of their number to take full charge of community affairs and to iron out conflicts that affected everyone. These people became the town administrators—the first secular government officials. Apparently they were elected democratically, and their primary job was to manage the irrigation system. But over the years they took on much wider responsibilities, so that more and more people were needed to sort out the increasingly complicated affairs of government.

Towards the end of the fourth millennium BC, several of the temple-towns had grown so large and diversified that they were turning into what we now recognize as cities. They had large populations, and although the great majority of the people were still engaged in agriculture, others had branched out into various occupations. There were priests, temple workers, government officials, teachers, craftsmen and artisans. Class divisions had also sprung up, with some groups and some occupations enjoying a higher status than others.

By this time, political rivalries among the budding cities had become fierce. Each one wanted to control as much of the irrigated land as possible, and to exert its dominance over neighbouring towns and villages. Power and prestige were treasured prizes, and the cities would gladly have wiped each other out to acquire them.

A standard of Ur depicts the people in peacetime going about their various trades.

Such ambitions produced another characteristic of civilization—warfare. Although the Sumerian communities shared a common language and culture, the people were loyal only to their own cities, each of which struggled to control the whole Mesopotamian valley.

The frequent threat of attack made it necessary for the people to pick the strongest and boldest among them as their military chief. He was called the "big man", meaning "king" in Sumerian. At first, the king was in charge only during times of warfare; once the danger was over he gracefully retired to his civilian job, and the regular government took over again.

But as warfare became almost constant, the job of king changed from a temporary position to a permanent one. Eventually the king could no longer be replaced by a decision of the people. His authority became entrenched and hereditary, so that the Sumerians lost their original, more democratic type of government. Thus one of the earliest lessons of civilization was that continual warfare could breed authoritarianism.

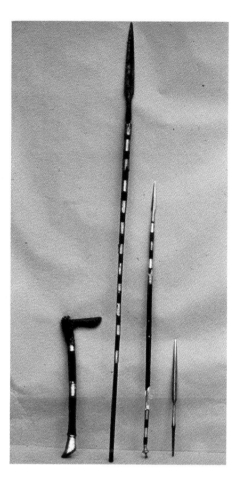

Among the earliest Sumerian weapons were spears and hatchets that came from Ur.

A standard of war shows men armed for combat and driving their vehicles off to battle. It is one of the earliest known works of art in which the wheel is represented.

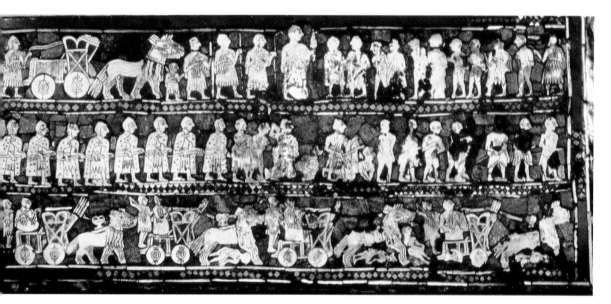

CHAPTER 3

INSIDE
THE GREAT WALLS

By about 3000 BC or earlier, several of the Sumerian towns had burgeoned into full-scale cities, each ruled by a king. Among the largest and most powerful were Ur, Kish, Uruk (called Erech in the Bible), Eridu, Lagash and Nippur.

These city-states, looming up on the horizon, must have seemed like a dazzling, spectacular mirage to the primitive nomads who happened to wander by. Huge, terraced temple-towers—called ziggurats—jutted up from their midst, and palaces, elaborate houses, markets, workshops, other temples and shrines, date-palm groves and gardens were clustered inside the walls. Surrounding the cities as far as the eye could see were acres of neat cultivated lands criss-crossed by irrigation canals and dotted with reservoirs. The Sumerians had come a long way since their arrival in Mesopotamia some five hundred years earlier.

When they were not busy fighting with each other, the Sumerians continued to display the remarkable ingenuity that had first spurred their rise. When faced with the need to transport food and other supplies over increasingly long distances, they turned to a new device—the wheel. Although it is not known if the Sumerians actually invented the wheel themselves or borrowed the

idea from others, they put it to widespread use. Carts on solid wooden discs were piled high with merchandise and rolled through the city streets, or they were used to bring the harvests in from the outlying fields, and to facilitate trade with neighbouring towns and villages. The wheel enabled one man to do the work of many and to distribute goods faster than ever before. This, in turn, permitted the further expansion of the city.

A detail from the war standard of Ur. By 3500 BC, Ur was a flourishing city.

Reconstruction of a huge ziggurat at Ur, which was built in very early times and then restored by Nebuchadnezzar II in the sixth century BC.

Games were highly popular among the Sumerians, and game-boards were works of art as well as playthings. This one is inlaid with lapis lazuli and red limestone.

A golden headdress remains intact on the skull of a lady-in-waiting found in the tomb of a queen of Ur.

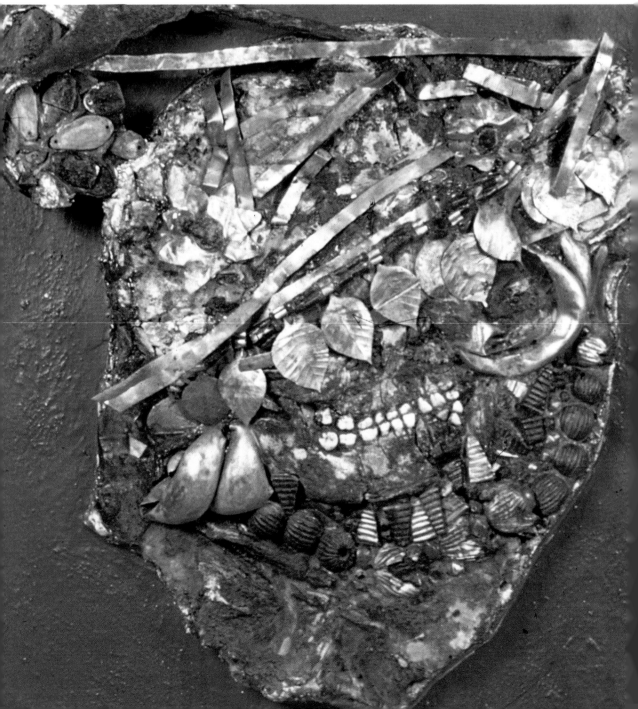

The Sumerians also advanced the art of writing, became expert traders, developed the sciences of mathematics and astronomy, as well as the practice of astrology, and divided up time into years, months, days, hours and minutes. They learned how to spin and weave fabrics of wool and linen. They made jewellery and tools out of copper and ornamented their clay vessels with beautiful paints and glazes. As early as 3000 BC, Uruk had foundries for smelting metals at very high temperatures, so that the people were able to forge such large equipment as ploughs. And all this was occurring at a time when Europe had not yet emerged from the Stone Age.

But the Sumerians were always preoccupied with war, and much of their energies were directed to military ends. Perhaps the most distinguishing feature of the Sumerian cities were the enormous defensive walls that surrounded them. Such walls helped keep the enemy out and were a protection against floods, but they also girded the cities and prevented them from expanding easily. As a city's population swelled, the people were jammed together more tightly within the rigid confines of the walls. A city that wanted more room had to break down part of its wall and rebuild it farther out, which was not an easy task. Thus the cities continued to be tightly knit units that could not sprawl unchecked into the countryside.

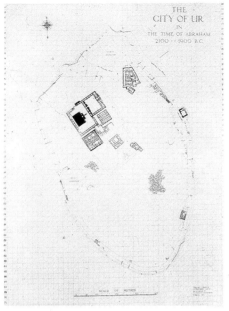

Map of Ur showing the city at its peak size, 2100–1900 BC, surrounded by a wall.

A lyre with a bull's head of gold and lapis lazuli was made in Ur in about 2500 BC.

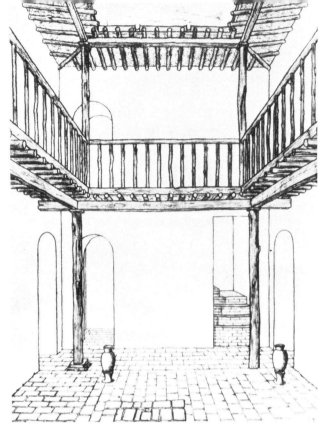

Restoration of a house in the residential quarter of Ur during the time of Abraham, about 2000 BC.

The oldest town

The most famous walled city of all time was not in Mesopotamia. It was Jericho—a lush and verdant oasis in the desert near the Jordan River, not far from the Dead Sea. In ancient times, this region was known as Canaan.

For a long time it was believed that the Mesopotamian city-states predated Jericho. But then in 1958, when archaeologists were digging deeper into the Jericho mound, they uncovered the remains of a remarkably ancient town that dated back before 7000 BC. At that early period, the Sumerians had not yet entered the Mesopotamian valley, and semi-nomads were first learning how to farm the hilly regions of northern Mesopotamia.

The early town of Jericho had several city-like features. It was large, covering about ten acres (four

hectares), and might have had as many as two thousand inhabitants. But, most amazing of all, it was surrounded by massive stone walls. Although the people had no knowledge of pottery-making yet, and apparently were not advanced enough to have domesticated any animals, they were using grinding stones and mortars and pestles to process their food. However, since all the people appeared to have been engaged in agriculture, Jericho could not actually be called a city yet, but rather an oversized, walled farming town. Apparently Jericho did not become a true city until after the rise of the Sumerian city-states. Generally, a city is defined as a place where people work at *diverse* occupations within a specific area, under a common government.

Archaeologists believe that the people of Jericho may have discovered agriculture well before 8000 BC, and that their original farming settlement may have been the oldest in the world. Certainly the region had many natural assets that would have stimulated the early growth of farming.

Separated from Mesopotamia by the vast Syrian desert, Jericho lay in a valley almost 1,000 feet (305 metres) below sea-level, and was surrounded by mountains 4,000 feet (1,220 metres) high. Although it was in one of the driest regions of the world, Jericho had its own spring—Elisha's fountain—which flowed at the rate of 1,000 gallons (3,785 litres) a minute. There was also another abundant spring nearby, and the presence of all this water made Jericho a green oasis in the midst of a barren desert.

The first people to wander into this lush, almost tropical wonderland may have settled down in rock shelters or in small caves near the springs. Later on, after they learned how to work the land and their settlement grew much larger, they built the giant wall that enclosed the cultivated lands as well as their precious springs.

This may have been the first time that any group of people actually walled off a portion of the earth and claimed it as their own, for the first Jericho wall dates back to before 7000 BC. Most likely the people put up the wall as a defence against nomadic invaders, marking the start of the age-old conflict between men who want to build fences and others who want to tear them down and roam the earth freely.

Over the millennia, Jericho grew into a full-fledged city, equal in size and grandeur to the Mesopotamian city-states. Its wall was rebuilt, strengthened and enlarged over and over again, until Jericho became one of the world's most impenetrable fortresses.

The city's enduring fame comes from the Bible, which relates the bloody tale of Joshua and the battle of Jericho. In about 1200 BC, when nomadic tribes of Israelites were attempting to make their way into the Holy Land, they ran head on into the great walled city of Jericho, which blocked their path. Since the only way to get past was by destroying Jericho, the Israelites, under their commander, Joshua, laid siege to the city.

This was a formidable task, for at that time Jericho was ringed by a double set of walls. The outside wall was 6 feet, 6 inches (2 metres) thick and nearly 33 feet (10 metres) high. Some distance inside this wall was a second wall, which was about $11\frac{1}{2}$ feet (3·4 metres) thick. The king, the patrician families and the wealthy merchants lived inside the walls while the peasants lived in mud huts outside the walls.

According to the Bible, the Lord told Joshua that he and his warriors must circle the city once each day for six days. On the seventh day they were to circle the city seven times, while seven priests blew on trumpets of rams' horns. The Bible says:

And it shall come to pass, that when they make a long blast with the ram's horn, and when ye hear the sound of the trumpet, all the people shall shout with a great shout; and the wall of the city shall fall down flat. . . .

So the people shouted when the priests blew with the trumpets: and . . . the wall fell down flat, so that the people went up into the city, every man straight before him, and they took the city.

And they utterly destroyed all that was in the city, both man and woman, young and old, and ox, and sheep, and ass, with the edge of the sword. . . .

And they burnt the city with fire, and all that was therein: only the silver, and

Excavations at the Jericho mound revealed that the city was much older than was previously believed. There is evidence that Jericho existed before 7000 BC.

Workers continue digging up the remains of Nippur, uncovering the city's ancient ziggurat. The various layers, or strata, date back to different periods in the city's history, with the oldest layer at the bottom.

the gold, and the vessels of brass and of iron, they put into the treasury of the house of the Lord.

Afterwards Joshua put a curse on Jericho so that it would never again be rebuilt, and the victorious Israelites marched past the ruined city into the Holy Land.

Such—according to the Bible—was the fate of Jericho. Today, archaeologists believe that it may not have been the Israelites who toppled the great wall of Jericho, but a natural phenomenon—an earthquake. The site of Jericho lies in a volcanic zone where there have been many seismic disturbances, and a particularly severe one may have occurred at about the time the Israelites were attacking the city.

Jericho was not the only ancient city whose inhabitants were totally wiped out by invaders. Such massacres happened all the time, so it is no wonder that cities surrounded themselves with the strongest, most massive walls they could build.

In the Sumerian city-states, the greatest danger was not from nomadic invaders but from other city-states. The rise of cities and the rise of warfare went hand in hand, and losers knew that either death, slavery or subjugation awaited them. The first of the Sumerian city-states to gain control over all Sumer was Kish. Next, Uruk held sway. Later on, Nippur conquered the whole region, and within a relatively short time, Uruk regained power. By about 2100 BC, Ur had taken control, but this turned out to be the last Sumerian dynasty in Mesopotamia.

Weakened by centuries of warfare, Ur and the other Sumerian city-states had no strength left. Outside enemies had come storming into the Mesopotamian valley, and the Sumerians were under steady attack from both the Elamites of Iran and the West Amorites, a group of

Semitic nomads from the Syrian and Arabian deserts. Both of these groups had coveted the riches of Mesopotamia for centuries, and they had made incursions into the area before. In about 2000 BC, the city of Ur fell to the outsiders, marking the end of Sumerian dominance in Mesopotamia.

The Amorites then drove the Elamites out of the area and invaded one Sumerian city after another, conquering them all. They replaced the Sumerian language with their own, but adopted much of the Sumerian culture once they settled down to live in the city-states. One of the smaller centres that they conquered was Babylon, a then nondescript town in southern Mesopotamia about fifty miles below what is now Baghdad. In the eighteenth century BC, an Amorite dynasty was founded here.

Once the Amorites were in control of the various Mesopotamian cities, they behaved just like the Sumerians: that is, they became rivals and fell to battling with each other for dominance over the whole region. But after Hammurabi ascended the throne at Babylon in about 1792 BC, he subdued all the warring cities and created a vast, powerful empire. From Hammurabi's time on, the Mesopotamian valley became known as Babylonia, and the old Sumerian civilization faded from memory.

Actually, the Babylonians did not bring about any radical changes in the culture of the Mesopotamian valley. Rather, they expanded and built upon the Sumerian culture. Their language was different and they worshipped different gods, yet they carried forward most of the myths, legends, political structures, technology, art and architecture of one of the world's first urban builders, the Sumerians.

Grandeur and squalor

By the time of Hammurabi, the Mesopotamian cities were displaying that combination of grandeur and squalor that has marked every large city down through the ages. Temples, palaces and large, extravagant homes existed side by side with hovels, for rich and poor alike were clustered together inside the city walls. The streets, which were unpaved, were pathways, strewn with garbage. Pedestrians had to be wary at all times, lest they be struck by flying loads of rubbish.

Most of the houses were rather drab-looking mud-brick structures, with no windows facing the streets. The only opening that could be seen by passers-by was a single, narrow entryway. All other doors and windows opened on to an inner courtyard that was not visible from the street, ensuring the utmost privacy.

Head of Hammurabi, king of Babylon, whose reign began about 1792 BC. Under Hammurabi's rule, Babylon became the centre of a powerful empire.

A typical house was either one or two storeys high and had adjoining rooms that formed a rectangle round the interior courtyard.

Some of the wealthier homes were amazingly sturdy and well built. When archaeologists dug up remains from the ancient city of Mari, which was conquered by Hammurabi in about 1760 BC, they found a 300-room palace with many walls still intact. In fact, they reported that many of the kitchens, pantries and terracotta bathtubs in the palace were in such good shape that they could still be used—some four thousand years after they were built!

Each of the Babylonian cities had a central marketplace where people could buy fruits and vegetables, meat and fish, clothing, household goods, and luxury items from other lands.

Apparently the people also frequented restaurants and taverns and congregated in the public square to watch wrestling matches, to gamble or to listen to stories. These squares became exciting entertainment centres and a major attraction of urban life.

The city people also enjoyed proverbs and wise sayings that reflected many of life's ironies. Among the favourites were these, as translated by Edmund I. Gordon in his book *Sumerian Proverbs*:

Who possesses much silver may be happy; who possesses much barley may be glad; but he who has nothing at all may sleep.

In a city that has no watchdogs, the fox is the overseer.

For a man's pleasure there is marriage; on thinking it over there is divorce.

Conceiving is nice; pregnancy is irksome.

The wife is a man's future; the son is a man's refuge; the daughter is a man's salvation; the daughter-in-law is a man's devil.

Friendship lasts a day, kingship forever.

The strong live by their own wages; the weak by the wages of their children.

Into an open mouth a fly enters.

The Mesopotamian cities were rich in literature and folklore that dated back to the early Sumerians. Undoubtedly the most famous creation of these ancient years was the *Epic of Gilgamesh*, a 3,500-line poem describing the wandering life of an early ruler of Uruk. The poem deals with such timeless themes as loyalty, courage and man's quest for immortality.

The Babylonian people were divided into three main social groups —the aristocracy, the ordinary citizens and the slaves. These divisions in society had begun to arise thousands of years earlier when the production of a stable food surplus first enabled men to channel their energies into other activities besides farming.

The aristocracy consisted of

Clay model of a sheep liver, inscribed as a guide to diviners, originating in southern Babylonia around 1700 BC.

wealthy landowners and priests, who served as public officials. Below them were the people who did all the day-to-day work—they provided food, built houses and worked as craftsmen and artisans.

Such jobs were also carried out by the large class of slaves, most of whom were prisoners of war. Free Babylonians could sell themselves or their children into slavery, if overwhelmed by poverty and hunger. It was an acceptable solution to their problems since slavery was not necessarily permanent: a slave could buy his own freedom. Furthermore, he had other legal rights, including the right to participate in business and to borrow money.

Hammurabi had drawn up a very elaborate and specific law code that tightly regulated the lives of the Babylonians. For a long time it was believed that this was the first written legal code in the history of mankind, but subsequent discoveries have shown that other, similar codes had existed before. None of the earlier codes, however, were as broad in scope as Hammurabi's, and it was his code that influenced much of the legal thinking of future civilizations.

Some kind of law code, written or otherwise, was a necessity after man's social structure became more complex and urbanization had begun. There had to be some way of guaranteeing orderly relations among large numbers of people, if only to avoid constant bloodshed and promote the healthy growth of the cities.

Hammurabi's Code was made up of about three hundred laws, a large number of which dealt with offences against property and land tenure. Laws regulating the family were next in importance. They focused on such matters as marriage, adultery, divorce, desertion, adoption, in-

heritance, incest and concubinage. Other laws dealt with trade and commerce, the administration of justice, penalties for assault, regulation of professional services, rates of hire and the ownership and sale of slaves.

Hammurabi's Code established a uniform pattern of justice throughout Babylonia, although by modern standards it was a very harsh justice, for it went by the principle of "an eye for an eye". For example, one provision says:

If a man has destroyed the eye of a man of the "gentleman" class, they shall destroy his eye. If he has broken a gentleman's bone, they shall break his bone. If he has destroyed the eye of a commoner or broken a bone of a commoner, he shall pay one *mina* of silver. If he has destroyed the eye of a gentleman's slave, or broken a bone of a gentleman's slave, he shall pay half the slave's price.

Hammurabi's code of laws was more detailed and comprehensive than any written legal code that pre-dated it. It strongly influenced the law codes of future civilizations.

It was very risky for a man to be a surgeon in Hammurabi's time, for the code stated: "If the surgeon has made a serious wound [incision] in a gentleman with a bronze knife, and has thereby caused the gentleman to die, they shall cut off the surgeon's hand." But if his surgery saved the gentleman's life, ". . . he shall receive ten shekels of silver. If the patient is a commoner, he shall receive five shekels of silver."

Workers who built shoddy houses were also taking great risks. The code said:

If a builder has made a house for a man but has not made his work strong, so that the house he made falls down and causes the death of the owner of the house, that builder shall be put to death. If it causes the death of the son of the owner of the house, they shall kill the son of that builder.

Nor did children dare rebel too violently against their parents, for the code said: "If a son has struck his father, they shall cut off his hand."

Revival of warfare

Although the Babylonians managed to preserve a high degree of order within their cities, they were far less successful in their external affairs. After Hammurabi's death, the empire splintered once again, and friction and warfare among the cities continued as before.

Among the people who had been forced to accept Babylonian rule during Hammurabi's reign were the Assyrians, a fierce warfaring people from northern Mesopotamia. Although they continued to be dominated by others for the next few centuries, they finally became strong enough to gain their independence in about 1350 BC. From then on, they were the feared and hated enemies of the Babylonians.

Time after time the Assyrians invaded and captured Babylon, but they were never able to hold on to their prize for very long. Then, in 689 BC, Assyria's King Sennacherib totally wrecked Babylon. All the inhabitants were killed and their houses destroyed. The temples and the ziggurat were smashed, and the debris was thrown into the canals. As a finishing touch, Sennacherib diverted one of the irrigation canals directly into the centre of Babylon, totally flooding the ruined city. But even that did not exhaust his rage. In pure malice, he loaded a ship with Babylonian soil and transported it north, where the soil was scattered to the winds.

Now the Assyrian capital, Nineveh, reigned supreme over Mesopotamia. Located on the banks of the Tigris River, Nineveh was probably the most warlike city in history. The people were broader and more muscular than others of that era, and they worshipped strength. They

Bronze gates of Balawat, Assyria, depict men armed with bows and arrows and other weapons marching off to battle.

Top left: *relief showing a warship belonging to Sennacherib, king of Assyria, who set out to destroy Babylon.* Top right: *a detail of irrigation.*

The capture of Lachish by the Assyrians portrayed in a relief. Under Sennacherib, the Assyrians conquered most of the lands of the Near East.

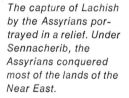

Wall slab portraying King Sennacherib's cavalry in the mountains comes from the king's palace at Nineveh.

prayed to huge stone idols of lions and bulls with eagle wings and human heads that represented strength, courage and victory. The priests encouraged warfare, perhaps even more avidly than anyone else, since they were supported by the spoils of conquest.

Nineveh was surrounded by monstrous walls that were more than 100 feet (30 metres) high and so broad that three chariots could be driven abreast across the top. As an added defence, moats were dug around the outside of the walls. The area inside was about 18 square miles (47 square kilometres), and the peak population was about 175,000.

The Assyrians were not as culturally advanced as the Babylonians and had copied much of their writing, literature, economic practices and legal ideas. Jealousy of the Babylonians' accomplishments probably had much to do with the Assyrian Sennacherib's brutality towards Babylon in the final siege.

Brutality was one thing at which the Assyrians excelled. Nineveh came to be feared as the "bloody city" because of the many atrocities committed by the Assyrian kings in their ruthless drive to conquer. In some of their captive cities they cut off the hands, feet, ears and noses of the inhabitants and put out their eyes. Other times they impaled people on stakes or skinned them alive. Sennacherib was said to have salted and packed the heads of his victims in baskets. Sennacherib himself was murdered by one of his own sons.

The Assyrians eventually conquered almost all the lands of the Near East and terrorized the people with their barbaric cruelty. However, they overextended themselves and could not control the far-flung lands of their empire. One by one, the suppressed nations rebelled. Towards the end of the seventh century BC, the Chaldeans of Babylonia and the Medes from the northern plateau region of Persia joined forces against the Assyrians.

Saracus, the last of the Assyrian kings, was besieged in his palace at Nineveh for two years until the Tigris flooded, undermining a river wall of the palace. The wall fell, and the invaders took Nineveh while the Assyrian king set fire to his own palace and died in the flames. Thus Nineveh and the Assyrian nation were wiped off the map. (Not all of their accomplishments had been negative, however. During the seventh century BC, the Assyrian

Reconstruction of the palace at Nineveh includes huge stone idols with human heads that represented strength, courage and victory.

king Assurbanipal amassed an immense library, which historians now call the single most important collection of cuneiform material ever found.)

Meanwhile, Babylon was being rebuilt. Under Nebuchadnezzar II, the ancient city was entering a new era of splendour and magnificence that far surpassed anything it had known before. During his 43-year reign—from 605 to 562 BC—Nebuchadnezzar turned Babylon into a cosmopolitan metropolis that could rival any of today's great urban centres.

Obsessed with a drive to build everything bigger and better than it had been before, the powerful king put up an abundance of temples, palaces and monuments, their brickwork all glazed and glittering in colours of red, blue, yellow and cream. He laid out wide, stately processional streets and built dams and reservoirs. To protect his newly built treasures, he surrounded the city with walls that enclosed a total area of over 100 square miles (259 square kilometres). This included the old city of Kish, as well as other urban centres that had been swallowed up by Babylon. In area it was the largest walled city of all time, and it contained about 300,000 to 400,000

Carving shows Assyrian King Assurbanipal enjoying a banquet. He was famed for his library, which contained a vast collection of cuneiform material.

inhabitants. These were more people than had ever been brought together in one place before.

Among Nebuchadnezzar's architectural wonders were the famed Hanging Gardens of Babylon. According to legend, he built them to please his wife, who was homesick for the green hills of her homeland. Babylon itself was very flat, so Nebuchadnezzar constructed artificial hills in the form of several large terraces that reached as high as the city walls. These were landscaped with trees, flowers, shrubbery and other foliage, and they looked like a great forest growing on a mountain.

Only one other sight could match the Hanging Gardens in breathtaking magnificence—the Tower of Babel. This was a colossal, multicoloured ziggurat that stretched almost 300 feet (91 metres) above

Above: *colourful enamelled tiles adorn the reconstruction of the magnificent Ishtar Gate in Babylon, built by Nebuchadnezzar II.* Left: *a reconstruction of the Hanging Gardens of Babylon.* Above right: *an artist's rendition of workers being driven from the nearly finished Tower of Babel as enemies attack.* Right: *all that remains of the South Palace of Nebuchadnezzar, where the fabled Hanging Gardens of Babylon once stood.*

the earth and was crowned with a golden roof. Nebuchadnezzar built the tower "to compete with the heavens" and to dazzle the world with his own power and majesty.

But Nebuchadnezzar was not a benevolent king. He forced his own citizens, as well as captive people, to build his spectacular creations, no matter what the hardship. The Jews especially despised him, for he had burned the Temple of Solomon in Jerusalem and forced them into exile in Babylon. The Jews were disgusted by the city's showy opulence, as well as by the thousands of temples and altars dedicated to strange gods. They regarded Babylon as the sinful "mother of harlots", and their loathing was mirrored later on in the many Biblical condemnations of the city.

As with all the great cities that had preceded it, Babylon's halcyon days did not last. The city declined after Nebuchadnezzar's death and finally, in 538 BC, it was captured by the Persians and became part of their empire.

Cities outside Mesopotamia

Although some of the world's first cities are believed to have arisen in Mesopotamia, this region did not hold its urban monopoly very long. Susa (in what is now Iran), Troy (Turkey), Mohenjo-Daro (Pakistan), Memphis (Egypt) and Anyang (China) were cities that emerged almost as far back as the urban centres of Mesopotamia.

Despite their vast cultural differences, these cities had many things in common. They were all surrounded by fertile farm lands that yielded the large food surpluses so vital to urban growth. Most of the cities developed in river valleys where the inhabitants could channel recurring floods to irrigate the land. Later on, they relied on river transport to exchange goods with far-off people. The strategic role of the rivers can be seen by the fact that both Ur and Uruk faded into insignificance after the Euphrates shifted its course and veered away from them.

Large defensive walls were a common feature of most ancient cities, and even though there were some open urban centres, cities were usually walled areas. Inside the walls, the people worked at a great variety of trades and lived under complex social, political and economic systems.

But it must be remembered that it had taken many thousands of years for these systems to evolve. From the beginnings of the agricultural revolution in about 10,000 BC to the rise of Jericho in about 7000 BC, some three thousand years elapsed. The emergence of the Sumerian city-states came after another four thousand years of evolution (*twice* the number of years that separate modern civilization from the days of the Roman Empire).

Excavations at Susa, Iran, revealed that the city was almost as old as the Mesopotamian cities.

Millennium after millennium, people had struggled with such problems as the periodic flooding of the Tigris and Euphrates, learning slowly, painstakingly, how to harness nature. It was out of this unending struggle that more complex social structures developed and cities eventually emerged.

"Cities" were synonymous with "civilization", since most of the learning, literature, science, technology, law and other advances of the people took place in the great urban centres. Although by far the greatest number of people were still engaged in farming, it was the minority in the cities who forged and fashioned world events.

But urbanization brought the bad along with the good. Wars, massacres, slavery, rigid class differences and despotic governments rose along with the cities, laying the foundation for all that was to follow in the next few thousand years.

The ruins of Tchoga Zambil, Iran, contain some remarkably well-preserved structures, including an arched gateway.

The city of Knossos on the island of Crete was in its prime between about 1700 and 1400 BC (known as its late period and from which most of its remains date), as urbanization spread north across the Mediterranean.

CHAPTER 4

THE GOLDEN AGE:
ATHENS AND ROME

The colossal splendours of Babylon were not to be found in early Athens. The Greek city-state—called a polis—seemed far more intent on building great minds than great monuments, and during the glowing years of its cultural supremacy in the fifth century BC it showed a casual disregard for material pomp.

Visitors to Athens—who had heard so much about the city's magnificent accomplishments — were stunned to see just an ordinary, overgrown, and rather dirty town. If there was something special about Athens, it was not apparent at first sight. This was far different from most other cities of that time, where the rulers made sure their achievements were visible to everyone.

Athens was not the first important city in Europe. As navigation improved and urbanization spread north and west from the Middle East and Egypt across the Mediterranean, the first European city grew on the island of Crete, south of the Greek mainland, in the seventeenth century BC. The metropolis was called Knossos, and it was renowned for one remarkable structure: its enormous palace. Covering about six acres (two and a half hectares) on top of a hill, the palace was a labyrinth of over four hundred rooms, halls, chambers, stairways

Knossos was known for its enormous palace, which contained over four hundred rooms. Shown are the ruins of the palace's south front.

This fresco of a bull decorated the north porch of the Palace of Knossos.

Reconstruction of one of the queen's rooms in the Palace of Knossos shows elaborate structure. Doors lead to a labyrinth of stairways, inner courts and other chambers.

and inner courts. In some sections it reached a height of four storeys. From its huge, unglassed picture windows, palace residents could keep an eye on the villas, houses, workshops and marketplaces below, as well as on the ships that sailed in and out of the harbour.

The people of Knossos were advanced enough to be concerned about sanitation. The city had a good drainage system and many refuse pits, and the better houses contained bathrooms with water closets.

While Knossos was at the peak of its development, urbanization was just beginning on the mainland of Greece. Among the small, fortified villages that were on their way to becoming significant powers in the ancient world were Sparta, Corinth and Athens. By the sixth century BC, Corinth had jumped into the lead and was the largest and richest trading centre in Greece. Sparta was more like a military training camp than a city, while Athens was gaining

distinction under its leader and lawmaker Solon.

Like other Greek cities, Athens based its growth on trade and commerce rather than on farming, for the rocky soil of the surrounding area could not produce enough to support a large population. But the Athenians were able seafarers, and they imported the extra food they needed in exchange for their wine, olive oil, wool and the exquisite ceramics that were in demand all over the civilized world.

Most of the Greek cities were inclined to set up new colonies as soon as their populations grew too large to feed. Corinth founded Syracuse and Corcyra as early as 734 BC. For a century and a half afterwards a steady stream of Greek colonists left other Greek cities to settle in regions from Spain to the Black Sea, spreading Hellenic culture wherever they went. Sometimes cities with just a few thousand inhabitants would send out colonies even though they were not overcrowded in the least.

Athens, however, was an exception. Lewis Mumford, one of the world's foremost urban experts and author of *The City in History*, has pointed out that

Athens, with its system of imperialist exploitation and overseas trade in pottery and oil, was not among the great colonizing cities. By keeping its citizens close to home, this city overpassed the limits of safe growth and increased its dependence on war and tribute for its continued "prosperity".

Athens' growth was hindered by an endless series of wars. Like the Sumerian and Babylonian urban centres, the Greek city-states did not get along with each other at all. They were physically separated by the hilly, jagged terrain, and they never established any kind of unified political system. Instead, their history was one of constant warfare, mainly with each other but also with an assortment of foreign enemies.

Athens did not soar to its greatest heights until after a devastating attack in 480 BC by the Persians, who practically levelled the Greek city-state. The Athenians eventually rallied and chased the Persians out of Europe altogether. Then they began the job of rebuilding their city. It was during this rebirth that Athens flowered into the world's most famous citadel of culture and learning. The city's intellectual achievements during these few centuries have never been surpassed, laying the foundation for the culture of modern Western civilization. Philosophy, science, architecture, art, medicine and drama are just some of the fields in which the Athenians excelled.

But perhaps the most vital gift that Athens gave to the world was the concept of democracy. By present standards it was a very limited democracy, but it flourished at a time when other cities were controlled by omnipotent kings or tyrants, many of whom claimed godlike qualities. In contrast, Athens was a centre of freedom where each

The roadway leading from Athens to its bustling port, Piraeus, was protected by a pair of long, thick walls.

people could vote. Excluded from citizenship were women, slaves, all foreigners and even the first generation of children born to foreigners. These disenfranchised groups accounted for the bulk of the population. The slaves alone numbered 100,000.

Such high percentages of slaves and non-citizens were common in all ancient cities, beginning with Ur and Uruk. What should be emphasized is that in the context of its time Athens was unusually advanced and progressive, even though it was more like an oligarchy than a true democracy. For the first time, political control was not based on wealth or social standing. To an Athenian, citizenship was more valuable than either of these.

Foreigners could neither become citizens, nor own land. They could, however, own businesses, and a great many foreigners were merchants, shopkeepers, bankers, craftsmen and artisans. Athenian citizens tended to look down on such work (in fact, on *all* work) because they prized a leisurely life in which they could cultivate their minds and their bodies. With income derived mainly from land holdings, slaves to do their work for them, and foreigners to handle most of the business and commerce, they were able to live the way they wished.

The citizens devoted much of their time to civic affairs, and they took turns serving as legislators and jurors. But there were poorer citizens, too, who had to work and could not afford the time off to fulfil civic duties. Pericles, who led Athens during its Golden Age in the fifth century BC, solved this problem by paying poor citizens from the public treasury during their periods of service.

Athens' limited democracy created a peculiar division in its popula-

individual citizen had an equal right and duty to take part in civic affairs.

This had not always been so. Until the time of Solon in the sixth century BC, Athens had been dominated by kings and aristocrats. But Solon drew up a series of reforms—including the abolition of serfdom and giving political rights to all property owners—that started Athens on the path to democracy. Solon's work was carried on by Cleisthenes, who in 506 BC (or thereabouts) proclaimed that all free Athenian citizens were equal, and that each one should have a voice in the government. Decisions were to be made directly by the people in the public assembly, which was held outdoors in the *agora*—marketplace. Such a system was possible only because Athens was small enough so that all the free citizens could come together in one place. As the Polis grew, this method became unwieldy.

From Cleisthenes' time on, Athens was ruled by its free citizens. The only flaw in this system was that the great majority of Athenians were *not* citizens and had no political rights at all. During the time the city was at its peak, about 290,000 people lived in Athens and its suburban ports of Piraeus and Phaleron. But only 40,000 of these people were citizens, which meant that less than one out of seven

tion. Most of the men who handled the city's trade and business and worked in the necessary, everyday occupations had no voice at all in the government of the city. For them, Athens could never be anything more than a source of money. At the same time, most of the men who controlled the government had little to say about the city's business affairs and, over the centuries, they became far removed from the "lowly" but vital activities on which the city's health depended.

This lack of cohesion sapped the city's strength, for Athens never really became economically self-sufficient. It grew too dependent on the tributes it demanded from lesser cities, as well as on the labour of foreigners. It could not stand on its own for very long and finally lost both its democracy and its independence to foreign conquerers.

But independent or not, Athens continued to produce men of brilliance, just as it had been doing since the sixth century BC. For a city that was no bigger in area than London's Hyde Park, it left the world a remarkable legacy of achievements.

Physically, Athens was not very impressive, especially in the early years before the time of Pericles. The original polis grew up on the slopes of a 492-foot (150-metre) cliff, high above the Aegean Sea. At the top of the cliff was a fortress-like area—the Acropolis—that provided protection for the village below.

The Acropolis was believed to be the home of many gods, but it also served as a fort until its destruction by the Persians in 480 BC. Then it was rebuilt as a sacred religious centre, harbouring a marble temple dedicated to the goddess Athena. This temple—called the Parthenon—is now considered one of the greatest architectural masterpieces in the world. Unlike most ancient structural wonders, the Parthenon was not built on a vast scale. In fact, it was rather small, measuring only 230 feet (70 metres) in length and 35 feet (11 metres) in height. Its beauty lay in the perfect harmony and simplicity of its style, and it soon became the model for all Greek temples. Another temple, the Erechtheum, was built on the Acropolis some years later and was separated from the Parthenon by a sacred street. Farther away was still another

The Acropolis, the ancient rocky citadel of Athens, lies at the top of a 492-foot cliff, overlooking the lower city stretching toward the Aegean Sea. Athenians built many of their temples and religious shrines on the Acropolis.

The architectural grace and beauty of the Parthenon—the marble temple dedicated to the goddess Athena—is still apparent as it stands amidst the ruins of the Acropolis. The temple has eight Doric columns in the front and rear, and seventeen along each side.

The Propylaea—the series of roofed porticos leading to the Acropolis at Athens—was built in the Doric style of architecture between 437 and 432 BC. The structure was never completely finished, and much of it was destroyed by invading armies.

religious sanctuary, the Propylaea, which won renown for its magnificent marble door. Statues of Athena and other sacred shrines and memorials also sat atop the Acropolis, so that each time the people made the steep pilgrimage to their temple-city, it was as if they were climbing right up to the heavens.

But if the Acropolis was a scene of breathtaking beauty, the city below was not. The streets of Athens were no more than narrow, winding alleys, lined mostly with flimsy houses made of unbaked brick. Anyone who wanted to break into one of these houses could just dig through the walls. Even flimsier houses than these existed—houses made of mud and wattle with thatched roofs that looked as if they belonged in some primitive village rather than in the most culturally advanced city of the ancient world.

The homes of the rich were not very different from the homes of the poor, except that they were somewhat larger and the furnishings were better. But the rich did not indulge themselves with many lavish possessions, and their clothing was so simple that it was hard to distinguish a rich man from a slave; all the Athenians dressed simply.

Statue of an Athenian man displays simple style of clothing worn by rich and poor alike.

The streets of Athens were unpaved, so that during the rainy periods they turned to mud and during the hot summers they turned to dust. But Athenians did not seem to care much about their physical surroundings, and they ignored such matters.

For a city of several hundred thousand people, sanitation was deplorable. As late as the fifth century BC, Athens had no orderly method for disposing of garbage and human waste. Yet such systems were not unknown. The Sumerian city of Ur had developed good sanitation facilities a few thousand years earlier, and the ancient city of Mohenjo-Daro could boast of bathrooms and toilets in every house. Crete, too, had bathrooms and water closets. But in Athens garbage and waste accumulated in the streets and in big piles along the outskirts

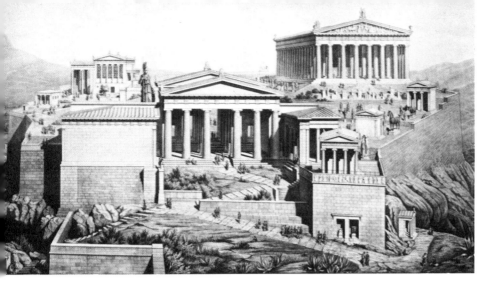

A reconstruction of the Acropolis as it might have looked near the end of the fifth century BC. At the front is the Propylaea, which served as the gateway to the Parthenon (right rear) and the Erechtheum (left rear).

of town. The stench and filth of these "municipal dumps" was indescribable, for all kinds of refuse was left here to rot—even unwanted babies.

Athens' backwardness in urban sanitation contrasted sharply with its advanced intellectual and cultural development. In the agora men clustered in small groups to discuss public affairs, debate with one another and philosophize about life. These discussions were part of the Athenian citizens' everyday activities, as necessary to them as food. The agora was always alive with talk; with people haggling over prices, negotiating business deals or just gossiping; with orators addressing the milling throngs; and with scoundrels looking for someone to swindle. The agora was the centre of intellectual ferment, and it also served as the gathering place for the public assembly.

When Athenians were not involved in civic affairs or debates, they were likely to be found in the gymnasiums, keeping their bodies fit. Athletes were as honoured as scholars, for the people prized both sound minds and sound bodies. Young men learned wrestling, spear-throwing, racing and ball games along with reading, writing and music. Athletic contests were held in arenas and gymnasiums just outside the city gates, and crowds of spectators were always on hand. The Greek stress on sports was reflected in the traditional Panhellenic games, which began in about 776 BC. These contests were the ancient forerunners of today's Olympic games.

Athenian citizens were able to devote themselves to such activities because of all their leisure time. Although they might have spent this time in carousing or in the pursuit of material comforts, as most other leisured classes did, Athenians preferred a more temperate, well-balanced life. Their unique blend of intellectual curiosity, political freedom, dislike of extravagant living, and free time spurred

Relief dating back to 490 BC shows muscular Athenian athletes playing a game resembling hockey.

them on to unparalleled creativity.

Athens produced some of the world's foremost philosophers, playwrights, statesmen, scientists, mathematicians, physicians, architects and artists. Socrates (*c.* 470–399 BC), Plato (427–347 BC) and Aristotle (384–322 BC) established a philosophical tradition that lasted well into the modern world. Plays written by Aeschylus (525–456 BC), Sophocles (496?–406 BC), Euripides (485?–406? BC), Aristophones (448?–380 BC) and other ancient Athenians are so timeless that they are still being performed today. They created a new kind of literature with their plays that were performed in poetry, accompanied by music and dancing before large groups of people. From 506 to 406 BC, Athenians wrote and produced well over one thousand plays; Sophocles alone wrote about one hundred.

Athens became famous for its schools of learning—the Lyceum, the Academy and the Cynosarges—where a rational approach to education was stressed. The Athenians had their gods, as all ancient people had, yet they did not attribute everything in life to the erratic will of the gods; they searched for the reasons why things happened and why people behaved as they did. In their quest for logic, they cast off many of the superstitions of the ancient world and encouraged men to use the full scope of their minds. They looked at life as it was, seeking rational explanations for everything and using concrete analysis. For example, in analysing the need for

Remains of the Theatre of Dionysus in Athens, where a great many plays were performed. The large, open amphitheatre was built into the slopes of the surrounding hill.

Bust of Athenian philosopher details his thick beard, moustache and curly hair. Philosophers and other learned men of Athens stressed a more rational approach to life than people elsewhere.

governments, Aristotle compared the laws of more than one hundred cities. Athenian physicians sought organic causes of disease, not mystical ones.

Unending warfare

But unfortunately there was no logic at all in the relationship between Athens and the other Greek city-states. Skirmishes and friction continued almost without let-up. When Athens grew more ambitious about adding to its territory during the reign of Pericles, it seemed as if the city might dominate the entire Greek coastal region. Athens' traditional enemy, Sparta, reacted in fury. This touched off the Peloponnesian War, which lasted from 431 to 404 BC and which was mainly between Athens and Sparta but eventually involved almost all the Greek cities.

At the start of the war in 431 BC, peasants from the outlying regions poured into Athens, seeking shelter behind the city's strong walls. Their presence resulted in severe overcrowding, and the already dirty city became more filthy. During the second year of the war a new disaster struck—the plague. The Athenian writer Thucydides, historian of the Peloponnesian War, described the city during this time:

Never before had anyone heard of such a pestilence and destruction. Human knowledge was helpless against this evil —birds and animals which normally feed on human corpses did not go near them, even though they lay about unburied. If, however, they did feed on them, they too died. The sick, half-dead of thirst, stumbled through the streets and beleaguered the fountains . . . the people became indifferent towards everything they had held in awe and respect.

Pericles died of the plague in 429 BC, but despite the loss of their leader and the effects of the epidemic, the Athenians managed to hold out against Sparta for another twenty-five years. Finally, in 404 BC, Athens collapsed, this collapse marking the end of its attempts at political domination.

The city continued to flourish as a cultural centre even when it was no longer politically powerful. Plato and Aristotle produced their great works after Athens' political decline. But in 338 BC, Athens was conquered again, this time by Philip of Macedon. Soon afterwards, Philip's son—Alexander the Great—did something that the Greek city-states had never been able to do for themselves: he united them within the empire he built, which included most of the civilized world, as it was then known to Western culture.

Ironically, it was not until after Athens lost its freedom that the city became more concerned about its physical appearance. The new emphasis on surface beauty went hand in hand with a decline in intellectual vigour. By the third century BC Athens was a more attractive city to look at, but its years of creative glory were over.

The rise of Alexandria

Alexander the Great, who had been tutored by Aristotle, spread Greek culture throughout much of the world. Wherever his armies went they planted the seeds of Greek learning, so that the influence of the small city-states radiated in all directions.

Although Alexander destroyed many great cities beyond repair, he was also a master builder. He laid the plans for more than seventy new cities in Europe, Asia and Africa. The most splendid was Alexandria in Egypt, which he founded in 331 BC. Built in a rectangular shape three miles (nearly five kilometres) long and a mile (1·6 kilometres) wide, Alexandria had as its focal point two enormous boulevards lined with trees. One ran the length of the city, the other the width, and the glow of their oil lamps illuminated the entire metropolis at night. The main buildings were made of marble, adorned with graceful columns and exquisite sculpture.

For a city that was carved out of nothing, Alexandria was an instant success. Located on the Nile at the crossroads of three continents, it rapidly became the commercial centre of the Hellenic world and then its capital. Egyptians and Greeks poured into the city, as did the Jews after they were granted equality with the Greeks. The city was one of the few places on earth where Jews were safe from persecution, and it was not long before Alexandria had one of the largest Jewish populations in the world.

Rich, powerful and cosmopolitan, and nourished by the intellectual heritage of Athens, Alexandria soon made its own contributions to the world's store of knowledge. Its Mouseion—or "seat of the Muses"—was a publicly financed centre for scientific research and education. It housed lecture halls, laboratories, observatories, a park and a zoo. Its vast library contained the entire body of Greek literature and the scientific works of the ancient world. All of the writing was inscribed on over five hundred thousand rolls of papyrus. It was in the Mouseion that Euclid and Archimedes did some of their research, made experiments and discovered theorems that were vital for the full flowering of the sciences many centuries later.

When the Arabs conquered Alexandria in AD 641, it was said that they used the remains of the library's vast collection as fuel to heat the public baths. According to an old and probably false legend, the Caliph Omar I felt that if the Greek works coincided with the Koran they were of no use and did not have to be preserved; if they differed, they were dangerous and had to be destroyed.

At the time that Alexandria was at its zenith, Athens was a declining force in the world and Rome was just beginning its ascent. The death of Alexander the Great in 323 BC (when he was only thirty-two years old) threw his empire into disarray and left a vacuum of power. Ambitious, aggressive cities now competed with each other in efforts to create empires of their own. Among the deadliest rivals were Carthage and Rome.

Carthage had established her supremacy on the seas, while Rome was building up a string of conquests in central Italy. Rome had begun as a village on the Palatine Hill above the Tiber River, in 753 BC. Over the years other settlements sprang up on the six surrounding hills, and by about 600 BC all of them had joined together.

This primitive village had no particular talents. Its people were not good artisans or craftsmen and they did not engage in much commerce. But they were good fighters, and they enriched themselves periodically with the spoils of warfare.

In about 510 BC the Romans overthrew their king and replaced him with two consuls who were elected by the noblemen or patricians for one-year terms. Later on, the franchise was extended to commoners as well. In order to ensure popular support from one election to the next, the consuls had to come up with crowd-pleasing policies. War was always a popular activity among the Romans, and the consuls urged their people on

to one conquest after another.

By about 300 BC, Rome was the mistress of central Italy, dominating an area of about 5,000 square miles (12,950 square kilometres) with nearly 400,000 inhabitants. Over the next few decades it also gained control over the southern part of the Italian peninsula, and by 264 BC the city was ready for conflict with Carthage.

The three Punic Wars between Rome and Carthage marked the beginning of Rome's attempts to extend its territory beyond the Italian mainland. After the final defeat of Hannibal and his Carthaginian forces in 202 BC, Rome's power was practically unchallenged. From then on, it was only a matter of time before Rome brought most of the Western civilized world under her dominion.

As parasitic as ever, Rome extracted heavy tributes from her world-wide provinces without giving back anything in return. The city held sway over an estimated 23 million people in Europe, plus another 32 million in Asia and Africa. Even cities as large and powerful as Alexandria were beholden to Rome.

But even though the Roman citizen might consider himself king of the world, living conditions in Rome itself were wretched. The city was as packed with people as the most teeming quarters of Calcutta or Hong Kong today, with more than one million people jammed into five square miles (12·95 square kilometres). One reason for this was that during the Punic Wars the Carthaginian forces had devastated much of the Italian countryside, destroying and burning whole villages and laying fields waste. Hundreds of thousands of displaced peasants and farmers poured into Rome. In the decades that followed, others were drawn to Rome in the hopes of finding a better life, or simply because they wanted to be a part of the city that ruled most of the civilized world. As the migration into Rome continued, a huge plebian mass was formed.

There was not much work for these people in Rome because most of the heavy chores and unskilled work was done by slaves. Why should wealthy Romans hire workers when there were so many slaves available from the far-flung empire? There was really no need for free workers on the bottom rung of the job-ladder. Further up the ladder was a middle class of civil servants, shopkeepers, teachers, doctors and artisans, but the poorer Romans had little hope of climbing to such heights.

The presence of large masses of

Left: *model of imperial Rome shows large public buildings clustered in the centre of the city, surrounded by miles of houses packed tightly together.*

Right: *Rome's domination and influence over much of Europe can be seen by this example of Roman architecture in Orange, France. The Roman-style theatre was built in the first century BC.*

unemployed people in the city was always dangerous, for a discontented mob might rise up in rebellion at any time. The Roman rulers were aware of this threat, and towards the end of the second century BC they passed a law that called for the sale of grain at less than market price to the residents of the city. In later years the grain was simply given away free each day to about 200,000 people. But this in itself had an adverse effect because it attracted even more peasants to Rome and added to the army of unemployed or semi-employed. In this respect, Rome was not too successful in dealing with the world's first large-scale urban unemployment problem.

To add to the plight of the poor, the cost of housing in Rome was extremely high. People were stuffed into rickety tenements that rose six to twelve storeys above the ground and housed as many as five hundred people. Most apartments consisted of a single room, usually no bigger than twelve square yards (ten square metres), for which the residents

paid dearly. Since the landlords were interested only in how much money they could get from the apartments, they constructed them as cheaply as possible. It was not uncommon for the taller buildings to collapse into a heap of debris. Fire was always a hazard; anyone trapped on the upper floors of a burning twelve-storey tenement had little chance of making it all the way down the steep, narrow wooden staircase.

The slum landlords usually leased their buildings to agents who collected the rents and squeezed additional profits from the hapless tenants. Many wealthy Romans, including the statesman and orator Cicero, made their fortune from these tenements. Cicero once bemoaned the condition of his own buildings, saying, "Two of my buildings have collapsed, in the others the walls are all cracked; not only the tenants, but even the mice have left."

The tall tenement buildings faced each other across narrow streets

Reconstruction of a Roman apartment building in existence during the time of Augustus. Wooden staircases made such buildings fire traps for people on the upper floors.

that were no more than ten feet wide. This meant that almost no sunlight filtered down to the lower apartments or to the winding lanes below. To alleviate such dreariness, the Emperor Augustus set a maximum limit of seven storeys for all new buildings.

Outside the city limits, fine houses could be had for far less money than the cost of an apartment in Rome. But lack of transportation made it vital for people to live in the heart of the city where they could be near their work (if they had any), and near the public entertainment centres such as the Circus Maximus and the Colosseum. Especially in the later years of the empire, the Roman rulers saw to it that the mobs were well entertained, in addition to being fed. They thought they could render the masses harmless through an unending supply of "bread and circuses".

Romans who lived on the farthest edge of the city could reach the Colosseum in about an hour's walk. Although the distance was only a little more than two miles (three kilometres), the streets of Rome were so congested that it was impossible to move quickly. This meant that anyone living outside the city limits would need well over an hour to reach the centre of activity— a commuting time that most Romans found unacceptable. Besides, the Romans seemed to like living right in the midst of the urban clatter and turmoil where they could feel the throb of the world's most powerful city.

By the first century BC, congestion in the streets had become such an

acute problem that Julius Caesar banned wheeled traffic from the city during the day. This meant that the streets were filled with noise at night when food and other supplies were wheeled into the city in wagons and carts. The ban on daytime traffic was renewed from time to time by the emperors, but, like many heavily

Battles between Roman gladiators were among the entertainment spectacles held at the Colosseum, a huge four-storey amphitheatre that seated about 45,000 spectators.

Ruins of the Roman Forum, where many public and judicial activities took place. It was here that Marc Antony delivered the funeral oration for Julius Caesar.

populated cities, Rome was never able to resolve its traffic problems. (Today, Rome seems to have unearthed Caesar's old plan: it has tried banning motor traffic from certain streets. Florence and Vienna have done the same.)

In contrast to the teeming streets and squalid tenements were Rome's magnificent public buildings, triumphal arches, statues and fountains. Inside the 50-foot-thick (15-metre) Servian wall that surrounded the city were 1,790 palaces, 11 public baths, 8 bridges, 36 marble arches, 37 gates, 6 obelisks, 2 circuses, 2 amphitheatres, 3 smaller theatres, 28 libraries, 4 gladiatorial schools, 290 storehouses, 254 public bakeries and 46,602 tenements.

Most of the city's streets were paved, and in about 312 BC a paved roadway—the Appian Way—was built to provide access to the city. Food and other provisions were transported to Rome over the Appian Way, which was so well built that it is still in use today, some 2,200 years after it was built.

Eleven aqueducts carried about 200 million gallons (750 million litres) of water into Rome each day. The city also had an excellent sewer system. The Cloaca Maxima, first constructed in the sixth century BC, provided Rome with sewers that surpassed all others in the ancient world. Parts of the Cloaca Maxima are in use to this day.

Rome's rich landowners, merchants, money-lenders, and land speculators indulged themselves with all the luxuries known to the ancient world. Unlike the Greeks, they adored palatial surroundings and usually had a lavish home in the country as well as one in the city. Some of these country estates had as many as fifty rooms, with bathrooms the size of a cottage. Glass windowpanes were introduced in these houses for the first time.

The children of the wealthy were educated by scholars brought from Greece, for a Greek tutor was considered a social necessity. Upper-class Romans learned Greek philosophy, art, architecture, literature and science, and they often adopted the Greek language as a means of showing off cultural superiority.

But in terms of political supremacy Greece's day was over, and Rome's was not to last much longer either. Rome had known nearly two centuries of peace, beginning with the reign of its first emperor, Augustus, in 27 BC. With most of the known world in Rome's grasp, there had not been anyone left to fight.

But, beginning in about AD 200, corruption and intrigue within Rome all but paralysed the government. Between AD 235 and 285, Rome had more than twenty emperors. Only one of them died of natural causes. Roman soldiers held the real power now, and they were becoming restless, periodically plundering the cities in the empire. At about the same time, the Germanic hordes started pressing in on Rome's provinces, some of which were dangerously close to insurrection.

Rome taxed its subjects heavily to

The Aqua Claudia was one of eleven aqueducts that carried a total of about two million gallons of water into Rome every day.

pay for the fighting, and the Roman armies took money, food and supplies at will. This only added to the unrest, particularly in the farms and villages that bore most of the burden. Rome had always neglected the rural parts of the empire in favour of the cities, and the peasants had no civic rights at all. When hard times came they fled to the urban centres, leaving the fields untended.

In the midst of this turmoil, another threat appeared—Christianity. The Roman emperors felt this new religion might undermine their power, and they persecuted the Christians without mercy. But even this failed to dampen the ardour of the religious converts, for Christianity seemed to offer the only salvation in a world that was becoming unendurable. The new religion swept Rome, and in AD 324 Constantine the Great made Christianity the state religion.

But Rome was plunging into an irreversible decline. After Constantinople (now Istanbul) was made the new capital of the empire in AD 330, the Roman mobs took to the streets and plundered their own city. Disorder and chaos were the rule over the next decades, until in AD 410, when the Visigoths broke through the last crumbling defences and sacked Rome. The Vandals completed the destruction forty-five years later, when they too pillaged the city. By the end of the fifth century AD, the once glorious city of Rome had only about 1,000 inhabitants, eking out their living in the wreckage-filled streets.

Rome was the first city to experience some of the major urban problems that are still with us today. Unemployment, overcrowding, poor housing, high rents, crimes, traffic problems and slums were all part of the urban scene when Rome was at its zenith. With almost all the

world's riches and power in its hands, Rome was still unable to provide decent living conditions for its own urban population, despite the efforts of a large civil service. In general, as long as the masses could be placated and amused, the Roman leaders were content to do little else for them. The same Rome that conquered the world and handed down so much law, architecture, and learning also introduced many of the most difficult problems still confronting city planners and administrators.

A model of Rome during the time of the Emperor Constantine, who in AD 313 issued the Edict of Milan, making Christianity the state religion.

Map shows blocks of apartment buildings in Ostia, the port of Rome, built about the second or third century AD. Ostia was originally founded in the fourth century BC as protection for Rome.

CHAPTER 5

AFTER THE FALL

After the fall of the Roman Empire, all of western Europe tumbled into chaos. Law and order broke down, so that there was no protection for anyone anywhere. City walls crumbled under repeated barbarian attacks. Trade and commerce ground to a halt.

Urban society all but vanished as people scattered to the countryside. From the fifth to the ninth centuries, cities shrank into towns and towns into villages as the people retreated into an agricultural way of life. Their only hope of security was to place themselves under the aegis of some powerful lord, working his land and serving him in return for his protection. Members of the nobility could also gain added security by pledging their fidelity to other, more powerful nobles. This was the start of the feudal system, in which the relationships between lord and vassal, master and serf, became rigidly defined.

By the time feudalism reached maturity, every man had his established place in society, with rights and duties inherited at birth.

The major unifying force in the medieval world was the Catholic Church, which had spread over all of western Europe. The power of the clergy matched, and often exceeded, the power of the nobility. These two groups formed the upper classes, while the serfs and other non-nobles made up the lower class. These groups were known as the "three estates". Although a promising peasant youth might enter the clergy from time to time, as a rule there was very little class mobility. In this feudal, agricultural world, a man's whole life was predetermined by the class in which he was born. While most other societies have also had rather rigid, non-mobile class systems, the stagnant, localized economies of medieval Europe made social mobility virtually impossible.

The literary and artistic achievements of the Greco-Roman civilization were practically forgotten during the early days of medieval Europe. The people remained isolated, both physically and culturally, from other parts of the civilized world. Almost everyone

The splendours of Byzantine architecture can be seen in the domed Hagia Sophia, originally a Christian church in Constantinople, built between 532 and 537 AD. When the Turks conquered the city in 1453, they converted the church into a mosque. Today it is a museum of Byzantine art.

Rome goes up in flames as Alaric I and his Visigoth army prepare to enter the fallen city in 410 AD. The invaders sacked Rome for several days.

was illiterate, and most of the technical and scientific advances of the Hellenic age had been lost. If it had not been for the monks in the monasteries, who knew Latin and hand-copied many of the ancient works, these masterpieces might have vanished forever.

Only one other offshoot of the Greco-Roman civilization remained, but it was a spectacular off-shoot indeed—the glittering city of Byzantium, heart of the Byzantine Empire. To non-urban, agricultural western Europe, Byzantium loomed as the only real metropolis. There art and literature flourished, proud basilicas jutted up towards the heavens, and merchants from Egypt, Babylon, Palestine, Hungary, Spain and Russia jostled each other in the busy streets.

Byzantium was a sophisticated, cosmopolitan city that radiated much of the culture of the Greco-Roman world. Located on the Bosporus, at the crossroads of Europe and Asia, the city had been founded in 667 BC by Greek colonists. But it did not rise to great heights until after the Emperor Constantine decided to make it the new capital of the Roman Empire in AD 330 and renamed it Constantinople. Today it is called Istanbul.

Fortress-like walls, built in the fifth century AD, protected the Christian city of Constantinople from barbarian invaders.

After Rome fell in AD 476 (when the last western emperor, Romulus Augustulus, was deposed), Constantinople was the only major city to survive the widespread chaos and upheaval. Standing as an almost impenetrable fortress against barbarians from the north and east, the city of Constantinople helped prevent the conquest of Europe by non-Christian groups. It remained a citadel of strength for almost one thousand years, holding aloft the torch for art, learning and commerce while western Europe slowly struggled out of its isolated torpor.

Most medieval Europeans, who spent their whole lives tilling the soil, could not even imagine a city like Constantinople, for there was nothing remotely like it in their own immediate surroundings. When the Crusaders from the west stopped off at Constantinople on their way to do battle with the Moslems for possession of the Holy Land that the Moslems had occupied, they were awe-struck by the dazzling metropolis. As one Crusader wrote:

All those who had never seen Constantinople before gazed with astonishment at the city. . . . They took careful note of the high walls and imposing towers that encircled it. They gazed with wonder at its rich palaces and mighty churches, for it was difficult for them to believe that there were indeed so many of them. As they gazed at the length and breadth of the superb city there was not a man, however brave and daring, who did not feel a shudder down his spine.

But the cultured, wordly-wise inhabitants of Constantinople had only contempt for these rough and ignorant Christian soldiers who disrupted the city with their unruly behaviour. The people of Constantinople actually had better rapport with the Moslems, whose

The old towers and walls of Constantinople still stand guard over the Bosporus. The sight of these majestic structures awed the Crusaders from western Europe who stopped off at Constantinople on their way to the Holy Land.

culture was more advanced than that of the feudal Christians.

Constantinople was a beautiful city. At its heart was a great thoroughfare called the Triumphal Way. Emperors returning from battle would enter the city through the magnificent Golden Gate and ride down the Triumphal Way, while thousands of spectators cheered. The city was filled with statues, obelisks, monuments and sparkling fountains. Water flowed into these fountains, and into the public baths and reservoirs, through the enormous aqueduct of Valens. When this aqueduct was renovated in the eighth century, it required almost three thousand workers, including two hundred whitewashers and five hundred brickmakers. The city's sanitation and drainage systems were excellent, making it one of the cleanest cities anywhere.

Constantinople's great libraries held thousands of volumes of Greek and Roman literature, in which the knowledge, culture and traditions of the ancient world were preserved. The city's huge stadium, the Hippodrome, was also a symbol of its Roman heritage. The stadium could hold 60,000 spectators in tier upon tier of white marble seats.

The Roman-style aqueduct in the background still stands in Istanbul (formerly Constantinople), Turkey. Huge aqueducts supplied the city with ample water for its public baths and reservoirs.

Constantinople was a brisk and busy place, alive with the hammering and clatter of workers, craftsmen and artisans, as well as the shouts of tradesmen. The people manufactured and exported woven silks, carved ivories, enamelled

The products of Constantinople's craftsmen were known for their lavish appearance and high quality. This water pitcher and cup and saucer illustrate the craftsmen's ability to work with ceramic, glass and bronze.

The splendour that was Constantinople can be seen in the Topkapi Sarayi, which was built as a palace but is now a museum.

Strongholds are filled with garments of silk, purple and gold. There is nothing in the whole world to be found to equal these storehouses and this wealth. The Greek inhabitants are very rich in gold and precious stones, and they go clothed in garments of silk with gold embroidery, and they ride horses, and look like princes. Indeed, the land is very rich in all cloth stuffs, and in bread, meat and wine. Wealth like that of Constantinople is not to be found in the whole world.

jewellery, ceramic wares and metal goods. In the different sections of the city various workers could be seen plying their trades. The coppersmiths and metal workers shared one noisy quarter, while the tanners and the leatherworkers went about their business in another. Each craft or trade was carried on in a separate section, and the finished products were in great demand throughout the civilized world. When kings or princes wanted the very finest works of gold and silver, mosaics, bronzes or sculptures, they commissioned them from Constantinople, the artistic capital of the world.

Visitors to the fabled city were astonished at the lavish clothing worn by the people, and by the extravagant way that they lived. As one chronicler wrote:

Both men and women adorned themselves with jewellery. Heavy gold and silver bracelets were favoured by the men, while the women liked pendant earrings and large filigree necklaces studded with precious stones and enhanced with enamels.

The houses in Constantinople were built in the Middle Eastern style. They faced inward, with windows looking on to an inner courtyard rather than out on to the street. Often these courtyards contained fountains, gardens, marble walkways, and statues, but they were visible only to the occupants of the houses. Just as in Rome and other large cities, the houses of the rich and poor could be found side by side. A run-down street lined with squalid wooden shacks might also boast a huge palace with marble columns and mosaics.

Such wealth was a tempting target for outsiders who yearned to plunder the city. Over the centuries Constantinople fought off attacks by the Saracens, Bulgars and Avars. After one fierce battle, the victorious Byzantine emperor punished the Bulgars by blinding thousands of their soldiers and sending them back home.

Ironically, the proud and splendid city, which had helped maintain Christianity in Europe for so many centuries, was brought to its knees in AD 1204 by Christian Crusaders.

The armies of the Fourth Crusade, which had started out for Egypt, were diverted to Constantinople instead. This switch had been planned by the Venetians because their own city was engaged in fierce commercial rivalry with Constantinople. They hoped to use the Crusade to conquer the city and bring it under Venice's control.

For three days and nights the Crusaders sacked, burned and plundered Constantinople. In an orgy of vandalism, the soldiers unleashed their envy of the city's wealth and power. Masterpieces of architecture, art and literature were destroyed, including the libraries where the Greek and Roman collections were stored. Many classic works were lost to the world forever because of the invaders' fury.

The Crusaders also disliked Constantinople because its inhabitants did not share their religious zeal. They wanted to convert the world to Christianity, while the people of Constantinople had no such ambitions. The Byzantine Christians tolerated other faiths and even allowed Moslem inhabitants to build mosques in the city. These mosques were among the first buildings to be destroyed by the Crusaders.

The invading armies did not leave anything untouched. As one horrified observer wrote:

They respected nothing, neither the churches, nor the sacred images of Christ and his Saints! They acted like enemies of the Cross! They committed atrocities upon men, respectable women, virgins and young girls. . . . They used Christians worse than Arabs use Latins, for at least the Arabs respected women.

What the Crusaders did not destroy they stole. Precious jewels, plates of gold and silver, chalices, mosaics, paintings, icons, golden candelabra and other costly,

exquisite works were carted out of Constantinople and brought back to other parts of Europe. The loot that was taken from the fallen city by the Crusaders was estimated to be worth seven times the annual revenue of England!

The Venetians maintained a very shaky hold on Constantinople until 1261, when a Greek dynasty gained control once again. But the damage had been done, and Constantinople would never again be as rich or as powerful as before. In 1453 the city fell to the Turks, marking the end of the thousand-year Byzantine Empire.

In contrast to the wealth of the city of Constantinople are hidden troglodyte dwellings (top) in Cappadocia, Turkey, where the early Christians lived for centuries.

After the Christian Crusaders destroyed Constantinople, and the city reverted once again to Moslem rule, there was a need for new palaces and mosques. The Blue Mosque, shown here, was constructed by Sultan Ahmed in the seventeenth century.

Arab culture booms

The only cities that matched Constantinople in wealth and power in the centuries after the fall of Rome were the Moslem centres of Baghdad (Iraq) and Córdoba (Spain). While most of Europe slept, Arab civilization was flowering. Between the seventh and thirteenth centuries the Arab world rose to its greatest heights of culture and learning.

Baghdad, the heart of the Arab empire, was built on the banks of the Tigris River in the eighth century by the ruling Arab caliphs to supplant the old capital of Damascus. More than 100,000 labourers, craftsmen and artisans were needed to build the new city, and the construction took four years. It was called "the round city" because it was circular in form, surrounded by double brick walls, a deep moat, and a third inner wall that was ninety feet (twenty-seven metres) high. At the centre of the city was the huge green-domed palace of the caliph, and next to that stood the great mosque.

Within fifty years, Baghdad grew into a splendid metropolis that thrived on international trade. The royal palace, which glittered with gold, silver and precious gems, was the scene of some of the world's most costly extravaganzas. Among them was the fabled marriage ceremony of Caliph Mamun in 825, during which one thousand large pearls were showered on the wedding couple while they stood on golden mats set with pearls and sapphires. Priceless gifts were given out to all the privileged people who attended the ceremony, and the palace was bedecked with exquisite treasures.

The city grew wealthy on world trade as hundreds of ships came in and out of its harbour every day. Baghdad's bazaars could offer such wares as silk and musk from China; spices and dyes from India; rubies, lapis lazuli and slaves from Central Asia; honey and furs from Scandinavia and Russia; and ivory, gold dust and slaves from east Africa. In exchange, Arab merchants exported fabrics, jewellery, glass beads and metal mirrors to the Far East, Europe and Africa.

Along with the acquisition of wealth came the acquisition of knowledge. The Moslems put a high priority on learning and greedily absorbed all the known science, technology and literature of the ancient world. Less than a century after the founding of Baghdad, the city's libraries were filled with the works of such classical scholars as Aristotle, Plato, Hippocrates and Galen, as well as medical and

Today one can still see remnants of the Moorish culture that flourished in Córdoba, Spain. The architecture of this mosque is but one example.

scientific treatises from India and Persia.

Building on this store of knowledge, and particularly on Greek philosophy, the Arabs went on to make their own vital contributions to learning. They made enormous strides in astronomy, mathematics and medicine and began the large-scale production of paper after its invention by the Chinese.

In 830 Caliph Mamun established his "House of Wisdom" in Baghdad. This was a combination library, school and translation office where thousands of volumes from other lands were translated into Arabic. Some famous Greek works that have been lost in their original language—such as Galen's seven books of anatomy—were preserved in the Arabic translation. In this way the Moslem cities of the Middle Ages kept alive the knowledge and culture of the Hellenic world and provided some continuity in the unsteady march of civilization.

Arab professionals—physicians, lawyers, teachers and writers—held a prominent place in Baghdad society. Learning was greatly respected, and large numbers of people were literate. One reason for this was that there was no organized priesthood in the Moslem religion, and people were urged to read the Koran themselves. Teaching someone to read was considered a good deed—a gift to Allah.

Schools and universities abounded throughout the Moslem world. Baghdad alone had thirty universities. In addition, the first schools for pharmacists were established there. Pharmacists had to pass a test to be certified, as did doctors. In 931 Baghdad had 860 qualified doctors.

Almost equal in wealth, splendour and learning to Baghdad was the Moslem city of Córdoba, the Arabs'

urban outpost in their European province of Spain. Córdoba had half a million inhabitants, 700 mosques, 300 public baths and 17 libraries, making it one of the most attractive centres of the Arab world. The royal palace alone had 400 rooms and apartments to house the ruling family and thousands of slaves and guards. Other cities such as Samarkand, Damascus and Cairo were also rich and lively centres of a vigorous Moslem civilization.

By the thirteenth century, however, the vigour of the Arab world had begun to decline. A long series of battles with the Crusaders added to internal decay had sapped its strength. Perhaps sensing this vulnerability, Genghis Khan and his Mongol hordes swept down from central Asia and slashed through the Moslem lands. City after city went up in flames. In 1258 the great metropolis of Baghdad was reduced to ashes.

Most of the Moslem world eventually recovered from these attacks, as it recovered from the ravages of the plague, but what remained was only a shadow of a once powerful and creative civilization. The Arab cities, like so many other cities of the past, had become a victim of that savage urge which has always led men to destroy what other men build.

The mosque here is just one of hundreds built by the Moslems in Córdoba. Even from this small portion it is easy to imagine the splendour that existed in the Moorish world.

CHAPTER 6

MEDIEVAL CITIES

During the long centuries when civilization was marching forward in Constantinople and the Arab world (as well as in China and India) Europe remained a primitive and backward region. Isolated from outside influences by a lack of trade and communications, most Europeans had little knowledge of what was going on elsewhere. Their world was bounded by the manor house and estate on which they worked, and perhaps by the small village nearby.

But even stagnation must end sometime, and by the tenth century there were signs that Europe was coming to life again. Advances in agriculture began to produce food surpluses, and this in turn gradually resulted in a rise in population that was vital for the revival of trade. Between the tenth and thirteenth centuries the population of the English counties climbed from about 1,200,000 to more than 2,300,000, while other regions experienced similar or greater gains.

Lewis Mumford, in *The City in History*, has emphasized that

The revival of trade is often taken . . . as the direct cause of the city building and civilizing activities that took place in the 11th century. But before this could happen, a surplus of rural products and a surplus of population were necessary to provide both goods for trade and customers to purchase them.

If the merchants themselves had been the chief occupants of the new cities, they would have had to take in each other's washing.

Most of the new towns began as local marketplaces and expanded along with the general rise in population and the growing abundance of goods for barter and sale. The urban revival was also spurred by the rediscovery of that age-old protective device, the wall—which made towns safer places to live and reduced the inhabitants' dependence on the protection of powerful lords. The towns also became convenient and safe stopping-off points for travellers who were making religious pilgrimages.

Turrets of the medieval walled city of Carcassonne, France. The city, restored in the nineteenth century, exists today as a splendid example of medieval architecture.

A triple wall rings the palace and other buildings that comprise the royal seat in Coburg, Germany. The structure has been in existence since 1012, when Coburg became the royal seat.

In addition, whole new areas were being opened up for settlement and farming as a result of technological advances. In the Low Countries land was being reclaimed from the sea by means of dikes; German woodlands were cleared and cultivated for agriculture; irrigation of crops was begun in Milan in 1179; and in France a group of monks drained an entire lake and transformed the exposed land into vineyards. The use of water mills and windmills became more widespread, and there were also advances in mining and metallurgy.

Europe was stirring, towns were growing, local trade was increasing, and commerce was becoming possible on a larger and larger scale. Eventually some of the more ambitious and adventurous merchants began making long trips to Constantinople and other points in the East to gather exotic wares. These long-distance traders brought jewels, mosaics, porcelains and tapestries back with them to western Europe, where the people were introduced for the first time to these splendours of the East. Only the rich nobles could afford such luxurious imports, but it was not long before other people were clamouring for imported items such as sugar and spices, fabrics and dyes.

These wares were sold at the traditional European fairs, held three or four times a year in different parts of the continent. They were sponsored by feudal lords who collected a tax on sales and in return guaranteed safe-conduct across their lands to the merchants and shoppers. People came from all over to attend these fairs, which were grand and exciting events.

But this system was not wholly satisfactory for the itinerant merchants. They still had to do a good deal of travelling from fair to fair, and the roads and by-ways were never safe. For added protection they banded together and travelled in groups, forming large caravans.

At length, the merchants' need for greater security and stability led them to settle in some of the better-located towns, situated either at the junction of main roads or on waterways. Here they sank their roots and established permanent businesses based on long-distance trade.

Such developments further stimulated the growth of the towns, many of which expanded into full-scale commercial cities. But these towns and cities were surrounded by strong defensive walls, so that as their populations swelled they tended to grow up rather than out. Tall wooden houses shot up side by side, with their upper storeys jutting out over the streets. The streets themselves were just alleys, usually no more than ten feet wide. Open sewers and poor sanitation added to the general filth, and all sorts of diseases were rampant.

Nevertheless, there was a saying that "town air makes free", since people who lived in towns were not directly under the arm of a lord. Although the cities were built on land owned by princes and noblemen and were subject to various fees and restrictions, the townspeople themselves were free to do as they pleased and to speak their minds— liberties that were unknown to the serfs who were bound to a lord's estate. If a serf could make his way to town, find work and pay town taxes, he could be liberated from feudal bondage.

The towns attracted many who sought freedom, as well as professional soldiers, younger sons of the nobility who could not inherit land, carpenters, leatherworkers, artisans, craftsmen, tradespeople, and returning Crusaders who did not wish to go back to rural life after having been exposed to the world's great cosmopolitan centres.

The Crusades themselves had a great deal to do with the rise of commerce and urban life, for they introduced thousands of European soldiers to the culture and technology of the more advanced East.

At the time of the first Crusade in the eleventh century, Paris and London were just large market towns. Within the next century or two (and after several more Crusades), London had grown to a city of over 40,000, while Paris gained more than 100,000 inhabitants. Venice and Milan matched Paris in size, and Genoa was about equal to London. But these were among the largest urban centres, for most medieval cities had between 5,000 and 40,000 inhabitants. Among the new commercial cities that became prominent during this period were Hamburg, Frankfurt, Innsbruck, Bruges, Ghent and Antwerp. More new towns were built in the twelfth and thirteenth centuries than in any other period between the fall of Rome and the Industrial Revolution.

A dynamic new social class emerged with the rise of these cities. Whereas in earlier times the nobility and the clergy held all authority in their hands, now the merchants, with their growing wealth and power, posed a challenge to the ruling groups. They fought to free their towns and cities from stifling obligations to local lords, and they secured charters that guaranteed them individual freedom and self-government.

As the cities evolved, new political and legal institutions also evolved. Eventually, most medieval cities formed their own town councils made up of representatives of business groups. They levied taxes and market tolls, made sure the streets and protective walls were kept in good repair, and maintained the town's militia. Legal problems and criminal matters were dealt with by another tribunal, so that the cities developed a whole new body of law.

The dangers and hazards of the medieval world had long ago made people aware that their survival depended on group or "corporate" strength. Individuals were too vulnerable if they stood alone. Merchants who had travelled together when they were itinerant pedlars

Sturdy walls gird the base of Mont-Saint-Michel, a medieval island village one mile off the coast of northwest France. Originally a monastery, the Gothic buildings were constructed in the thirteenth century by the order of Saint Michael.

continued to band together in the towns and cities. They formed merchant guilds that regulated their business and provided all of them with economic protection. In the early years, when the merchants were not yet imbued with the capitalistic drive for high profits, their guilds tried to guarantee fairness to all. They made sure that nobody cheated the public; they protected craftsmen, shopkeepers and each other from unfair competition; and they guarded against the disruption of the town's business by outside influences.

The craftsmen, too, had their guilds. Leatherworkers, blacksmiths and other master craftsmen each had their own associations that regulated production and set up standards of high-quality workmanship. In addition, guilds also had rights. In the case of the craft guilds, the most important one was the right to control trade.

Men who belonged to the same guilds were more than just business associates, for the guilds also served as fraternal organizations. The members ate and drank together, per-

formed plays, built schools, hospitals and chapels, helped each other in times of trouble and even established such welfare benefits as health and old-age insurance. A man's whole life was tied up with his guild.

Religion, too, was a potent, all-encompassing and highly visible force in medieval life. Every city, town and village could be spotted from afar by the soaring spires or towers of its churches.

In the cities the expansion of trade and industry provided the money to build magnificent churches. The Gothic style of architecture—a style that had emerged in France in the twelfth century—soon became characteristic of the medieval church (and of the medieval city as well).

Gothic style emphasized height. It featured tall spires, pointed arches, long, slender columns and ribbed vaulting. Flying buttresses, or stone supports, were built against the outside walls to help support the vaulting. Among the most striking features of the cathedrals were the large numbers of exquisite stained-glass windows depicting religious stories.

The building of the Gothic cathedrals was an expression of religious faith. So many people participated in these undertakings that they were really communal efforts. In Chartres, France, for example, many of the townspeople hitched themselves to carts to help pull stones to the cathedral because they wanted to have a personal role in building their place of worship. Most of the construction work on such jobs was done by the guild members, who also set the high standards of craftsmanship.

Among the first of the great Gothic churches to arise was the

An everyday street scene in a medieval city is depicted in this illustration from an old manuscript.

Merchants and craftsmen did a thriving business in many medieval towns, such as Bruges, Belgium, site of a splendid guildhall. Their guilds provided protection from unfair competition and generally regulated business practices.

Left: *shoppers examine merchandise at a medieval cloth market. In the fourteenth century in Florence alone, there were about 30,000 textile workers plying their trades.*

Right: *the single spire of Strasbourg Cathedral in France soars 466 feet. Built between 1015 and 1439, it is a masterpiece of Rhenish architecture. In the sixteenth century its astronomic clock was added.*

The massive Cathedral of Notre Dame in Paris, built in the twelfth century on the Île de la Cité, is predominantly Gothic but bears some traces of Romanesque design.

Cathedral of Sens, in France, which was consecrated in 1168. The vast and spectacular Cathedral of Notre Dame in Paris was begun in the middle of the twelfth century, and the famous cathedrals at Amiens, Reims and Le Mans went up in the thirteenth century. Such massive structures took many years to complete. Amiens Cathedral was under construction for sixty-one years.

The Gothic style of architecture spread to cities in England, Germany, Italy and elsewhere in Europe during the thirteenth century. Among the most famous examples are Westminster Abbey and Canterbury Cathedral in England, Cologne Cathedral in Germany and Milan Cathedral in Italy.

The task of building these churches was an education in itself. Major architectural problems had to be tackled and solved, and the knowledge thus gained was applied to civic buildings as well. Town and guild halls, hospitals, schools and belfries were also constructed in the Gothic style, so that the medieval cities were indelibly stamped in the Gothic mould.

The churches and their public squares were situated right in the heart of the urban scene. Town halls and other civic buildings were also centrally located, so that the medieval city had a clearly defined core. Because of the protective walls that surrounded them, the cities did not just spread out haphazardly. Most of them remained small in area. Generally there was no place in the medieval city that was more than half a mile from its centre, which meant that all inhabitants were within walking distance of each other.

In later times, many of the cities began to expand far beyond their walls, so that the walled-in section became the "inner city". Some of these walled "inner cities" still stand, such as the Cité in Carcassonne, France, which was restored in the eighteenth century. Not all of the medieval cities, however, had walls.

The majestic Canterbury Cathedral looks out over the city that serves as the spiritual centre of the Anglican Church. The cathedral was built between the eleventh and fifteenth centuries. The tallest tower, which was finished last, rises to a height of 235 feet.

Some, like Bruges, Belgium, apparently never found it necessary to enclose themselves for protection.

Throughout Europe church-building reached its zenith during the thirteenth century, while the expansion of cities and towns was also progressing rapidly. Some historians now feel that this century marked a high point of urban civilization. Cities were stable and well-organized, largely because of the guilds and the corporate way of life; many of the cities were self-governing; many had representative political institutions; there were no sharp class struggles; and there was relatively little crime and violence. Perhaps equally important, the people took great pride in their work. Unlike ancient Athens or Rome where the people loathed all forms of toil, the inhabitants of the medieval cities accepted work as a necessary part of a good life. They did not have slaves to do the work for them, which in itself was a startling departure from earlier times. From Sumer to Babylon to Rome, slaves had always formed a large part of the urban populations.

According to Lewis Mumford,

In certain respects, the medieval town had succeeded as no previous urban culture had done. For the first time, the majority of the inhabitants of a city were free men; except for special groups, like Jews, city dweller and citizen were now synonomous terms. . . . Though the social structure of the town remained a hierarchical one, the fact that a serf might become a free citizen had . . . brought about an increasing measure of social mobility.

But by the end of the thirteenth century subtle changes were already taking place in the economic and social structures of the cities—changes that stemmed largely from a growing desire for profits.

Prior to this time, most medieval merchants and businessmen had shown little interest in the profit motive. Moderate earnings had satisfied them. They liked the protection of a guild-regulated economy and they took the Church's ban on

People, horses, dogs and goats congregate in the narrow streets of medieval Siena, Italy, in this painting by Ambrogio Lorenzetti entitled The Effects of Good Government on the City *(a fresco in the Palazzo Pubblico). Open, arched doorways and windows are a striking feature of the architecture of that period.*

usury very seriously. (Christians were forbidden by the Church to charge interest on money they lent.)

But, as trade and commerce expanded in the twelfth and thirteenth centuries, it had become necessary for merchants to borrow money to finance long-distance and long-term ventures. Since Church restrictions had prevented Christians from becoming money-lenders, Jews took over that occupation. Jews could not own land, nor could they belong to guilds, which meant that money-lending was one of the few trades open to them.

For years the Jews were the bankers in many European cities. But as the thirteenth century wore on, a more capitalistic spirit gradually took hold of the merchants and businessmen. Christians began to overcome their earlier qualms about making high profits, and growing numbers of them became large-scale bankers and investors.

As the profit motive became more important, the guild system itself did not work as well any more. A widening gulf divided the merchant elite from lesser tradesmen and shopkeepers. The craft guilds grew more and more restrictive, charging high membership fees and setting down such narrow entry requirements that they became more like exclusive clubs than broadly based associations. Guild members were the privileged upper stratum of workers, and rigid divisions had grown up within the guilds as well. Only a few could become master craftsmen now, with the other workers held down in the lower ranks. In addition, the members began flouting guild regulations. They charged as much for their goods as possible, and they often engaged in unfair competitive practices. The corporateness of the medieval city was eroding, leaving in its wake burgeoning class struggles, competitiveness and individualism.

Medieval class structure

By the fourteenth century, the urban middle class was clearly divided into three main groups. There was an upper-middle class of wealthy bankers and merchants; a middle group of professionals, such as doctors, judges and notaries; and a lower-middle class of small merchants, skilled artisans and craftsmen.

The population of fourteenth-century Florence, for example, was divided in the following manner: out of about 90,000 inhabitants there were some 1,500 nobles, 600 notaries, 60 physicians and surgeons, 80 money-changers, 75 knights, 1,500 foreigners, traders and transients, 10,000 school-age children, and 30,000 workers in textile trades. The city also contained 110 churches and 200 workshops for the woollen trades, as well as 30 hospitals with more than 1,000 beds. This was a far better ratio of hospital beds to people than many modern cities have, and it was due mainly to the efforts of the Church. Many of the Holy Orders devoted themselves to caring for the sick and the poor and built hospitals in every town and city.

Such charity was sorely needed, for the urban poor were numerous. They kept pouring into the cities in increasing numbers, seeking opportunities that were rapidly shrinking as urban society grew more stratified. This problem of the poor migrating from the rural areas to the cities — usually lacking the skills necessary to earn a living in an urban setting — was not a unique feature of the Middle Ages. Cities as old as Ur and Babylon were confronted with it, and the problem reached critical proportions in ancient Rome. The dilemma is much the same today, for cities as diverse as New York, Calcutta and Buenos Aires are staggering under the heavy influx of poor, unskilled migrants from rural areas.

In many of the medieval cities the poor were forced to live outside the city walls because rents within them had soared beyond their means. Since the supply of space inside the walls was so limited, it was also very expensive.

In earlier times, city houses had been laid out with orchards, gardens and courtyards, providing plenty of open space. This partly compensated for the lack of good sanitary facilities. But by the fourteenth century many of the open spaces had been built on. Sheds, workshops and enlarged houses now stood on land that had once been reserved for gardens; even cemeteries were built upon.

Such overcrowding made the cities filthy, for most of them never developed good sanitation. Thus, as the Middle Ages wore on, the cities grew increasingly dirty. Rivers and streams were fouled with wastes, intensifying an age-old pollution problem that still plagues us today. By the end of the fourteenth century, the English Parliament passed what may have been the first anti-pollution law. It forbade the throwing of filth and garbage into streams, rivers and ditches.

Such a measure did not stem from a sense of aesthetics, because people then did not necessarily equate cleanliness with beauty. There was little stress on personal hygiene, and in some of the northern or remote regions of Europe the people never removed their clothing from November to April. In parts of the Balkans, peasants sewed themselves into their shirts and jackets for the winter.

Medieval people did realize, however, that there was some connection between filth and disease and that polluted water might make people sick. This health problem was intensified by the fact that the cemeteries were located in the heart of the city, often next to the wells

A painting of beggars by Breughel the Elder shows the misery of life for the poor and the disabled in medieval Europe.

containing the city's water supply. Underground seepage from the cemeteries sometimes contaminated the drinking water, causing severe illness and many deaths.

Housing conditions, too, had become less healthy by the fourteenth century. As houses were enlarged, it became customary to have many interior rooms without windows. These stuffy chambers retained heat well, but they lacked fresh air and sunshine. Furthermore, the houses were usually so overcrowded that when disease struck, everyone in the household caught it.

There was no such thing as privacy during most of the Middle Ages. Bedrooms were often set up as dormitories, housing not only the owner's family but the people who worked for him as well. Apprentices and journeymen often lived in the house of the master craftsman who employed them, just as clerks and other helpers sometimes lived in the merchants' homes. These employees became part of extended families that also included maids and other domestic servants. Sometimes the maids slept on trundle beds that were pulled out from under the master's and mistress's bed and stationed right alongside it.

All the people in the household ate together, and the master and his helpers usually conducted their business in shops that were attached to the main house. A man's home might also be his workshop, store and counting-house, for there were few divisions between home and work. Only a small number of crafts were carried on in workshops that were isolated from homes. These were the noisier trades, or ones that required special facilities, such as iron-making, glass-making, milling, and in some cases, weaving and dyeing.

By the later Middle Ages, the wealthier urban families had begun to develop a sense of privacy. They started taking their meals and entertaining separately from their employees, and at night they retired to a private bedroom. The gulf between a master and his workers grew wider as the master cut himself off socially from those in his employ. The relationship between the two groups became more distant and formal, culminating in rigid class distinctions between masters and workers.

The groups also came to be divided by differences in education. Business dealings had become very complex, particularly in the Italian city-states where merchants had devised such intricate schemes as holding companies, credit transfers and marine insurance. Young men entering business needed far more education than just reading, writing and arithmetic. Knowledge of law, government and diplomacy was an invaluable aid in the business world, so the wealthier urban classes began sending their sons to universities. By now the universities were placing less stress on theology and more on practical education.

The wealthy classes as a whole became more worldly and sophisticated, paying less attention to the hereafter and more attention to the "here and now". They sought money, power and fame, and many of them grew rather cynical about the teachings of the Church. This was partly because they were developing a more individualistic approach to life, and partly because the Church itself was becoming worldly and corrupt.

The Church had grown as materialistic as any of the urban nouveaux riches. It hungered for more money and land and often devised unethical means of acquiring them. Even the popes took part in the corruption. Some popes sold Church offices to make money, and Pope Alexander VI (pope 1492–1503) openly flouted canon law by acknowledging that he had two illegitimate children, Lucrezia and Cesare Borgia. Anti-clerical feeling grew stronger, with more and more Christians becoming convinced that priests were ignorant and monks immoral.

But this did not mean that the people were growing more tolerant of other religions. On the contrary, their prejudices hardened into hatred with the passage of time. Animosity towards the Jews was inflamed by the fact that so many Christians were in debt to Jewish money-lenders, and the merchant and craft guilds wanted to restrict Jewish economic activities. Throughout the Middle Ages Jews were repeatedly driven out from different countries, beginning with their expulsion from England in 1290 to their expulsions from Spain in 1492 and Portugal in 1497.

Jews had never enjoyed the full rights and privileges of other city dwellers and had usually lived in their own section of town by custom rather than law. The Church's Lateran Councils of 1179 and 1215 prohibited Christians from living among Jews, and in the thirteenth century Spain became the first European country to confine Jews forcibly to ghetto areas. By the sixteenth century this practice had spread to almost every city on the continent.

The Jewish ghettos were like small cities tucked inside larger cities. They were enclosed by walls, and their gates were locked at night and during Church festivals. During the daytime the inhabitants were allowed to venture out, but they had to wear badges or hats that identified them as Jews. Aside from the fact that the Jews had to pay exorbitant taxes,

their ghettos were very nearly autonomous. The people passed their own laws regulating business and other activities, and they had their own legal institutions, schools, guilds, hospitals, recreational facilities and charitable institutions.

Since the ghettos could not expand outward, they became heavily congested. Unusually tall houses were built to ease the overcrowding, but this only aggravated the unhealthy living conditions and increased the danger of fire. It was not until after the French Revolution that most of the ghettos were opened up, although some eastern European countries retained their walled-in ghettos until the twentieth century.

Top: *the Lateran Council of 1215 forced Jews to wear a badge or some form of identification that set them apart from the rest of the population and that brought ridicule and insult. At various times throughout their history, Jews were assaulted, confined to ghettos or expelled from their countries.*

Bottom: *the streets of fifteenth-century Florence can be seen in this painting of the martyrdom of Savonarola, a reforming friar who opposed the corruption of the Church and who was eventually burned at the stake.*

The Plague and the cities

The steady growth of city life and commerce during the Middle Ages was impeded—and very nearly halted—by one of the greatest natural catastrophes in history—the Plague. Called the "Black Death", bubonic plague raged through Europe during the fourteenth century and lingered until the seventeenth.

The cities were the hardest hit. Overcrowded and dirty, with hopelessly inadequate sanitation, they were fertile breeding grounds for the rampaging disease. Epidemics struck one city after another with terrifying swiftness, creating hysteria among the inhabitants and bringing business and social activity to a standstill. The most virulent and devastating outbreak occurred around the year 1348. The wealthier people fled the cities for the comparative safety of the countryside, but most of the others had no place to go. They stayed in the cities, and all too often they died there.

The Black Death came, and went, and came back again, terrorizing people on and off over the course of the fourteenth century. By the fifteenth century, the disease had lost much of its virulence, but it took another hundred years before the population of the European cities climbed back up to where it had been before the first epidemic. And the disease still returned at intervals for about another hundred years.

Despite the ravages of the Plague, the cities of fourteenth-century Europe spawned a cultural awakening that lasted until the early years of the sixteenth century. This was the Renaissance—a time when classical Greek and Latin works were rediscovered and individual self-expression and creativity flourished. The great masterpieces of art and literature created during the Renaissance have been admired down through the centuries.

The spirit of the Renaissance may perhaps be traced to the social and economic changes that were taking place in the medieval cities. The corporateness of earlier times had been replaced by a desire for individual achievement and personal gain; the self was no longer subordinated to the group. This new urban spirit may have been more selfish and less innocent than the old, but it was also a spirit in which individual genius could blossom.

In the cities, aspiring artists, poets and sculptors began coming together, drawing inspiration from each other's works and seeking out patrons to finance their undertakings. Throughout the world and throughout history, cities have always served as gathering places for the avant-garde, and most new cultural and intellectual movements have come into being in the cities.

The Renaissance began in Italy in the fourteenth century and spread north. It was centred in the Italian city-state of Florence, but all the major Italian cities shared in the cultural outpouring. Not one, however, could match Florence in producing men of great genius. Between the fourteenth and the sixteenth centuries Florence was the home of such painters as Cimabue, Giotto, Masaccio, Fra Angelico, Fra Filippo Lippi, Uccello, Botticelli, Benozzo Gozzoli, Ghirlandaio, Signorelli, Leonardo da Vinci, Raphael and Michelangelo. Among its sculptors were Ghiberti, Donatello, Luca della Robbia and, again, Michelangelo. Its architects included Brunelleschi, Michelozzo, Bramante and . . . Michelangelo. Writers such as Dante, Petrarch, Boccaccio, Pico della Mirandola and Machiavelli put their unique stamp on the ideas of the age.

The cities provided far more than just a stimulating environment in which these artists could live and work. They also provided the wealthy patrons of the arts—men who had made their fortunes in banking, commerce and industry. Italian cities such as Venice and Genoa were among the richest in Europe because of their strategic location in the Mediterranean basin —the cross-roads of world trade. Other Italian cities, including Florence and Milan, had first grown wealthy by serving as distribution centres for goods imported by sea. Later, Florence became one of the foremost banking centres in Europe.

With their early prosperity, the Italian cities also acquired political power and virtual independence, so that by the fourteenth century they were generally more advanced than other European urban centres. The Italian cities had developed the intricacies of commerce and business to an unparalleled degree, and their merchants, bankers and businessmen were worldly and well-educated.

Those who had accumulated great riches could show off their wealth by commissioning sculptures, paintings, bronzes and stained glass from the most renowned artists of their time, and by bestowing these great

works on the Church. It may be that these wealthy businessmen were simply trying to buy their way into heaven, but in the process they were financing the cultural flowering of Europe. Without their wealth, many of the exquisite and costly masterpieces of the Renaissance could never have been produced.

By the sixteenth century, the artists themselves achieved a high social standing. This was a significant change from the earlier medieval years when painters and sculptors were treated like any other craftsmen. A superb artist ranked no higher than a superb carpenter or shoemaker, for art as such had no special status. Individual genius in art was not recognized then, and artists were just ordinary guild members.

But with the growing individualism of later times, artistic genius was

A feeling of Renaissance life in Florence is shown in this section of the painting of Saint Peter Healing the Sick, *attributed to the Renaissance painters Masolino and Masaccio.*

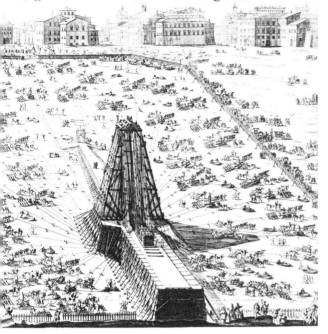

The obelisk in Saint Peter's Square, Rome, was a product of the Renaissance. It required nearly a thousand people (left) *to erect the monument, which still stands* (right).

not only recognized but highly prized. This, in turn, spurred artists on to greater heights, for if they were successful, fame and glory awaited them. A gifted artist could rise to the top of society regardless of his family background. Uccello's father was a barber, Fra Filippo Lippi's was a butcher and Botticelli's a tanner, but the artists were judged by their own talents rather than by the status of their families.

Art became far more humanistic and realistic than before, losing much of its symbolic, other-worldly quality. Artists strove to capture the human personality on canvas, as well as the human likeness. Merchants who commissioned paintings wanted to be able to recognize themselves (although preferably in an idealized, beautified form) and hoped to leave their painted likenesses for posterity. In this way they could gain a kind of immortality in the mortal world.

Florentine art set the standard against which all other works of art were measured. Florence's only rival in this regard was Venice, an even wealthier, more powerful commercial city that had developed its own distinctive art style.

Later on, the Renaissance spread to other European cities in Germany, France, England and Spain. The artists, writers and scholars— Edmund Spenser, William Shakespeare, Christopher Marlowe, Desiderius Erasmus, François Rabelais, Michel de Montaigne, Miguel de Cervantes, El Greco and Lope de Vega—are all products of the European Renaissance.

Along with the rebirth of art and literature came a growing (and typically nouveau-riche) desire for social refinements. The "proper" urban Renaissance man was a well-rounded gentleman, at ease in any company and able to carry on a lively conversation on just about any subject. He was a man who had read *Galateo*, or *The Book of Manners* (published around 1558) and heeded its many rules, such as:

Everyone should dress well, according to his age and his position in society. If he does not, it will be taken as a mark of contempt for other people;

Refrain as far as possible from making noises which grate upon the ear, such as grinding or sucking your teeth;

A man ... will take care not to get his fingers so greasy as to dirty his napkin with them, because the sight of it would be unsavoury to others.

Nor is it polite to wipe them on the bread;

Anyone whose legs are too thin, or exceptionally fat, or perhaps crooked, should not wear vivid or parti-colored hose, in order not to attract attention to his defects;

Wit should be like the nibble of a sheep rather than the bite of a dog, for if it were to bite like a dog, it would not be witty but insulting;

A man should never boast of his birth, his honours or his wealth, and still less of his brains . . . as many people do;

A man must . . . not be content to do things well, but must also aim to do them gracefully.

The Renaissance was a period when Europeans were thirsting for more knowledge, culture and sophistication. But at the same time, the Renaissance cities were experiencing an increase in violence and cruelty. The rise of individualism had been accompanied by a rise of aggression and competition in everyday life. The most popular entertainments of the time were bawdy comedies or brutal sports tournaments where spectators could delight in the savagery. Lawlessness was rampant. At night thieves and murderers lurked in the dark city streets, preying on passersby. If the criminals happened to be caught, they were treated with as much bestiality as they had shown to their victims: they were tortured or mutilated in the public square. Thus the Renaissance was a time of great contrasts, when urban people were reaching towards a more beautiful and elegant way of life, yet their cities were becoming increasingly violent. A comparison might be made with the United States of today—an enormously rich and technologically advanced nation, whose cities have grown so dangerous that people are moving away from them.

By the sixteenth century, when the Renaissance gradually faded, European cities had undergone striking changes. Politically, socially and economically, they were far removed from the cities of the thirteenth and fourteenth centuries. Most of them had lost the representative institutions of their medieval years, and oligarchies of rich merchants and property owners monopolized control. But the era of cities as comparatively independent political powers was nearly over, for Europe was entering a new age in which powerful monarchs would gradually consolidate their control over cities and localities.

Nevertheless, it was the cities that had been responsible for the cultural reawakening of Europe, for the Renaissance had its roots in urban society. The rise of cities and the growth of trade had exposed medieval Europeans to foreign cultures and new ideas, ending the rural isolation that had followed the fall of Rome. The early medieval cities had offered freedom from feudal ties and created a new middle class, while in later years these cities spawned a spirit of individualism and self-awareness.

A rendition of an ideal city by Italian painter Piero della Francesica. As always, there is a striking contrast between the order of the ideal urban setting and the chaos of reality.

CHAPTER 7

CITIES
OF THE NEW WORLD

The thrust to expand trade and commerce grew so strong by the later Middle Ages that adventurous Europeans rushed to explore every new route and market. Christopher Columbus's accidental discovery of the New World came about because of his desire to find a shorter trade route to the East Indies. In the course of his voyages he also proved that the earth was round, but this goal was secondary to his main goal of opening up new trade routes.

Columbus was followed by other explorers and adventurers who were drawn to the New World both by the lure of the unknown and the possibility of great riches. Gold and silver existed in abundance in the virgin lands, and the Indians used these precious metals as commonplace, everyday items.

To the Europeans, the American Indians seemed like backward, ignorant savages who had no legal or moral right to the treasures they owned. Viewing the Indians as sub-human creatures who worshipped strange gods, the explorers had no qualms about slaughtering them and stealing anything that might be valuable in their own "civilized" world.

It came as a shock to the Europeans to learn that some of these Indian tribes had highly advanced civilizations of their own, centred around elaborate cities. When the Spanish explorer Hernando Cortes marched up into the Mexican mountains in 1519 with about four hundred foot soldiers, some one thousand five hundred horsemen and several cannon, he came upon one Indian city after another. But the prize he sought was a city rumoured to be the grandest of them all—the capital of the Aztec Empire.

For weeks the explorers climbed onward and upward until at last they reached 7,000 feet above sea-level. Then on November 8 they saw it for the first time—Tenochtitlán, the shimmering Aztec capital, set like a radiant jewel on an island in the midst of Lake Texcoco. White towers and pyramidal temples jutted up from its midst, looming above the lush green foliage and thickly blooming flowers that surrounded the island metropolis.

A scale model of Ten-ochtitlán, the capital of the Aztec world. The model stands in the Museum of Anthropology of present-day Mexico City.

A view of the model of Tenochtitlán as it must have looked to the Spanish explorer Cortes when he sighted the city.

A front view of the pyramid of the Aztec god, Quetzalcóatl, who represented goodness and light opposing evil and darkness.

The city's temples and public buildings were covered with a hard white stucco that glistened in the sunlight, and the main avenues were smoothly paved with a cement-like finish. The highest point in the city was the royal hill of Chapultepec, crowned with a giant palace where the Aztec emperor Montezuma lived.

Cortes and his men were welcomed to the city by the Aztecs, who feared that the Spaniards might be related to their white-skinned, bearded god Quetzalcóatl. The Indians led the soldiers into Tenochtitlán over three thirty-foot-wide (nine-metre) causeways that connected the island metropolis to the surrounding land. Each of the causeways contained a bridge that could be lifted if the city wished to cut itself off from the mainland.

Lake Texcoco itself was a saltwater lake, so the Aztecs had built aqueducts that carried fresh water into the city from other nearby mountain lakes. As the Spaniards advanced into the heart of the city they saw that it was a crowded, bustling place. Later they estimated that the population was about 300,000 making Tenochtitlán larger than the largest European city of that time.

As described by William Prescott, the renowned nineteenth-century authority on Aztec society, the Spanish soldiers were led down a grand boulevard that stretched from one end of the city to another. At the centre they were met by Montezuma himself, riding in a canopied litter that blazed with jewels. The royal litter was borne on the shoulders of the Aztec nobles, since the Indians, despite their many accomplishments, had not yet discovered the practical applications of the wheel.

As befitted a great monarch, Montezuma was dressed in splendid finery. He wore garments of exquisitely embroidered cotton, topped by a cloak embroidered with pearls and emeralds. On his feet were golden sandals decorated with precious gems, and on his head was a feathered crown of green plumes that fell lightly down his back.

During a brief ceremonial meeting, Cortes presented Montezuma with a chain of crystal beads, and afterwards the Spaniards were led to their lodgings. On the way they passed the fine houses of the Aztec nobles that lined the main boulevard of Tenochtitlán. These houses were built of red or whitewashed stone that came from nearby quarries. Most were sprawling residences just one floor high, but some rose to a height of two storeys. The flat roofs were protected by stone parapets, so that every house was also a fortress.

The soldiers passed pyramidal temples, canals that glistened in the sunlight, and spacious market squares where goods ranging from jade and rubber to honey and vanilla were sold. Everywhere the Spaniards turned they were dazzled by the sight of flowers. In such beautiful surroundings even the simple mud and reed homes of the poor took on a certain charm. In many ways, the Aztec capital was reminiscent of the ancient Sumerian and Babylonian cities, for the architecture of the homes and the temple-pyramids was similar. Cortes and his men were astonished by what they saw, for the Indian city was nothing at all like the dark, overcrowded medieval cities that they were used to in Europe.

Tenochtitlán had no shops or stores as such, but every five days thousands of agricultural products and handcrafted goods were brought together for sale in the marketplace. Such markets were set up regularly in all of the Aztec cities, and they resembled the international fairs of Europe.

Indians from all the outlying lands came to the Aztec cities to attend the fairs, selling their own products and buying others, so that the cities were overflowing with people during these times. The biggest fairs were held in Tenochtitlán, where separate quarters were set aside for every kind of handicraft or product. Goldsmiths sold their wares in one section, and potters, jewellers, painters, feather-workers, stone-cutters, hunters, fishermen, fruit-sellers, florists and chairmakers each had sections of their own. Cottons, dresses, tapestries, curtains, coverlets, toys and trinkets, weapons, razors, mirrors and medicines were also sold at the fairs.

Trade was carried on partly by barter and partly by a type of currency that consisted of bits of tin cut in the form of a T, bags of cacao containing a specific number of grains, and gold dust.

Although the Aztecs owned slaves, these captives were used mainly for domestic service and heavy labour, and as religious sacrifices to the bloodthirsty Aztec gods. The Aztecs practised human sacrifice on a large scale. Near the entrance to Tenochtitlán was a rack that held about 100,000 skulls of young men and women who had been captured during wars. (Only the young were sacrificed.)

This statue of the Aztec goddess Coatlicue is but one example of the outstanding work done by Aztec stonecutters.

Slaves were not relied upon for most types of industry because the Aztecs took pride in doing their own work. Their attitude could be summed up in the words of one noble who advised a young Aztec: "Apply thyself, my son, to agriculture or to feather-work, or some other honourable calling. Thus did your ancestors before you. Else, how would they have provided for themselves and their families? Never was it heard that nobility alone was able to maintain a man."

The most respected occupation among the Aztecs was that of merchant. These traders travelled to the most remote corners of the Aztec Empire and beyond, buying and selling goods wherever they went. Like the early European merchants, they usually travelled together in armed caravans for protection against attack. This was necessary because there was frequent in-fighting among the various states that made up the Aztec confederation, as well as warfare with outsiders. Tenochtitlán exerted its supremacy harshly. Even more than Rome and Athens, Tenochtitlán lived as a parasite on the surrounding territory, exacting great tribute and wealth from her conquered enemies.

The Aztec merchants served a dual purpose—they also acted as spies for their emperor and princes in Tenochtitlán, supplying them with information about the far-flung provinces and about the inhabitants of other lands. Often they became trusted advisers of the monarch, exerting political and economic power in Aztec affairs. Their position in society was somewhat analogous to the European bourgeoisie, who stood between the upper class of nobles and priests and the lower class of ordinary workers, farmers and craftsmen. Thus, in some ways,

sixteenth-century Aztec society was evolving along similar lines to medieval European society.

Cortes and his men were housed in the mammoth palace of Axayacatl, which had been built by Montezuma's father fifty years before. The palace was spacious enough to accommodate Cortes's whole army at once, and it was strongly fortified by a thick stone wall studded with defence towers. The rambling, one-storey royal building was divided into roomy apartments decorated with gay cotton draperies and furnished with elaborately carved wooden stools, floor mats and beds of woven palm leaf. Cotton coverlets were draped over the beds, and canopies hung above them.

Montezuma's palace was even larger and far more grand than his father's. It was built of red stone and decorated with marble sculptures. The ceilings were made of intricately carved wood, and the walls were hung with feather-work draperies in an array of dazzling colours. Clouds of incense wafted through the enormous rooms, and there was enough gold, silver and precious gems on display to suit the tastes of any luxury-loving potentate.

Montezuma was obsessed with cleanliness. He is said to have bathed at least once a day and changed his clothes four times daily. After he had worn an outfit once, he gave it away; only fresh, new garments could touch his royal body. His palace contained more than one hundred baths that were supplied with water from a far-off reservoir, and each of Montezuma's many wives had her own private apartment and bath in the palace.

The royal palaces, temples, and fine homes of the upper class made Tenochtitlán a showcase of urban splendour. Such was the city that Cortes himself called "the most beautiful in the world" and "the Venice of the Aztecs". But after spending six days as a guest in the lovely city, Cortes made a captive of his host, Montezuma. Later on, when the Aztecs rose up against the Spanish garrison, Montezuma tried to pacify his people and was fatally wounded by a stone that one of them threw. The Spaniards were chased out of the city after suffering severe losses, but months later they returned to fight again under their leader, Cortes.

In brutal, hand-to-hand combat, they forced their way back into Tenochtitlán, levelling every house they passed. In August, 1521, after more than ninety days of bitter fighting, the Spaniards captured and completely destroyed the magnificent Aztec capital. Upon its ruins they built Mexico City.

Tenochtitlán was not the only large city in the New World. Farther south in what is now Peru was the huge metropolis of Cuzco, capital of the Inca Empire, which extended from what is now Ecuador in the north to Argentina and Chile in the south.

Cuzco, a city of about 200,000, was the religious, cultural, intellectual and commercial centre of the tightly knit Inca nation. ("Inca" was actually the name of the Peruvian Indians' royal chief, rather than the name of the people, but the term came to have a wider meaning.)

The Incas had developed a strictly regimented, communal society in which virtually all the means of production, distribution and exchange were in the hands of the state. This system stemmed from practical necessity since the soil in the Andean mountains of Peru required vast irrigation systems and terracing—works that could be accomplished only by people labouring together under strict discipline.

The Inca Indians built up Cuzco into the flourishing capital city of their empire. They were outstanding engineers and architects and artists, especially in such crafts as weaving and ceramics.

The Incas had little individual freedom, either in their work or their other activities, for almost every phase of their lives was regulated. Marriage and child-bearing were controlled by the state, and each family unit was granted land by the state in proportion to the number of people to be fed, clothed and housed. This land was not *owned* by the family, because private ownership of land was unheard of; the family just held a portion of the earth and worked it as part of one

A restoration of Inca buildings, including the Temple of the Sun.

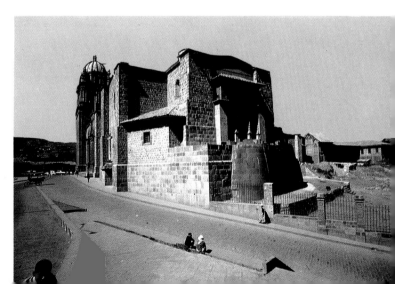

A wall still standing in San Domingo, Peru, shows the huge stone blocks that the Incas sometimes used in their constructions.

big agricultural system. Each family had enough land to provide a reasonable livelihood in return for a reasonable amount of work. They also spent time cultivating state and church lands to provide surplus food for those who were too busy to farm or were handicapped, disabled or elderly.

Although individualism was suppressed, the system was not as stifling as it might have been, because the state allowed for a good deal of leisure time. There were more than 150 holidays or rest days during the Incas' working year, which meant that they had far more free time than the peasants who tilled the soil in medieval Europe.

The vast majority of the Incas belonged to the lower, labouring class, while the small upper class—under their royal chief—took charge of governing the empire and administering justice, welfare services, military affairs and religious services. Although they were a hereditary, privileged class, they were more like a bureaucracy than an aristocracy. They were expected to perform their functions efficiently and could be punished for neglecting their duty or overstepping their powers.

The Inca Empire, which extended over 350,000 square miles (900,000 square kilometres), was governed from the capital city of Cuzco in a beautiful mountain valley 10,000 feet (3,000 metres) above sea-level. Although most of the houses were made of adobe and roofed with straw thatch, the massive public buildings were marvels of stone-masonry. Walls, palaces, administrative offices and temples were made out of huge square blocks of very hard stone, so perfectly sanded down and close-fitting that they looked almost like a solid sheet of rock.

City walls were made out of enormous stone blocks, each of which weighed several tons and had a diameter of more than sixteen feet (nearly five metres). Without having any knowledge of the wheel, and without the aid of horses or oxen, the Incas had managed to transport these massive blocks, shape them to perfection, and fit them together to form gigantic fortifications. The only tools they had to work with were primitive bronze levers and chisels, copper axes and stone mallets. The construction of the Sacsahuamán citadel outside Cuzco required the labour of about twenty thousand men working almost a hundred years.

In the heart of Cuzco was the Temple of the Sun, a huge structure whose stone walls were covered with gold and silver plate. The temple garden was adorned with solid gold replicas of stones, plants and animals, in homage to the Sun God.

Cuzco was both the religious and the educational centre of Inca society. Upper-class boys from all parts of the empire were educated over a four-year period in what could be called a university or teaching house in Cuzco. The students learned theology, philosophy, literature and history from professors who lived in the school and gave a

planned course of lectures. These professors were held in great esteem, and disciples flocked round them just as disciples had flocked round Socrates and Pluto in ancient Athens.

But the Inca civilization in Cuzco never reached its full flowering, for the city met the same fate as the Aztec capital, Tenochtitlán—it was demolished by the Spaniards. Under the leadership of an illiterate ex-swineherd named Francisco Pizarro, a troop of under two hundred Spanish adventurers invaded Cuzco and plundered it in 1533. A year earlier, the Spaniards had captured the Inca chief, Atahualpa, in the city of Cajamarca. He tried to buy his release by offering them a fantastic sum—a whole room filled almost to the ceiling with pure gold. Atahualpa's men had taken the treasure from temples and palaces all over the Inca Empire and brought it to their imprisoned leader. When it was not quite enough, Atahualpa added some seven hundred sheets of gold that had been part of the Temple of the Sun in Cuzco. The Incas had no idea of the value of all this gold in the European markets, for they themselves did not use it as a means of exchange. To them it was just a lovely shimmering metal that could easily be shaped into vessels, plates and ornamental objects. The roomful is estimated to have been worth $8 million (£3 million).

Pizarro took all the treasure, melted it down and gave each of his men a gold bar weighing between 50 and 100 pounds (22 and 45 kilograms). Then he had Atahualpa killed in the main square of Cuzco, after first seeing to it that the Inca chief was received into the Roman Catholic faith. (Cortes had also tried to convert the Indians to Catholicism and could never understand why they were so resistant.)

In 1536 the Incas rose up against Pizarro's occupation of Cuzco, and for the next year the city was a battlefield. When it was all over, the only objects left standing were the massive stone walls of the temples and palaces. The city of Cuzco was no more.

With Cuzco and Tenochtitlán both destroyed, the New World lost its two major urban centres. America was not to see cities of such size or splendour again for another three hundred years.

The outpouring of so much gold and silver from the New World was not an unmixed blessing for Europe. The abundant treasure caused a severe inflationary spiral in which prices went up much faster than wages. The working class grew poorer, and as a result there were periodic bread riots in many of the European cities.

An engraving depicting a meeting between the Incas and the Spaniards.

North American cities are born

It was not until the seventeenth century that the first small towns and villages began to dot the northern landscape of the New World. The Indians of the north had never been city builders like the Aztecs or Incas, and the first urban settlements were not begun until after the arrival of the Europeans.

These immigrants settled along the Atlantic coast, where they tried to recreate the kind of towns they had left behind. They were not trying to build a new and different civilization, but rather to implant familiar European settings in the New World. The changes they sought were social and political; they had no wish to change the basic culture of their original homeland.

In the early days, for example, the Dutch settlement of New Amsterdam looked just like a busy commercial town in Holland. The people built sturdy brick houses with roofs of coloured tiles that they had brought with them from Europe. Small gardens and orchards surrounded most homes, and the town had several windmills and a canal. But after the British captured the town in 1664 and turned New Amsterdam into New York, its physical appearance gradually changed and it began to look more English.

In general, British settlers built replicas of their own home towns, and the Dutch, French and Spanish did the same. Whatever changes evolved stemmed from differences in terrain and climate, the availability of raw materials and the need to adapt to local conditions. It was such factors as these that made the towns uniquely "American" after a while, even though they did not start out that way.

As with the leading European cities, the young American towns thrived on commerce. The five largest urban centres were also the major ports of the New World, for trade was the biggest occupation in the seventeenth century.

The five main ports—New York, Boston, Philadelphia, Newport, and Charles Town—served as the nerve centres of the budding American colonies. They were the cultural and intellectual capitals, as well as the hub of business activity, and they expanded quickly as the century wore on.

The ships that sailed into the American ports brought far more than just material goods. They brought news of all that was happening in Europe and beyond. They brought word of the latest in business, politics, art, drama and music; they brought new, sometimes revolutionary ideas about government and religion; and they brought the most advanced theories in medicine and science. In short, they brought civilization to a country that was being carved out of the wilderness.

But expansion also created the same types of urban problems that plagued the European cities. Poor

A watercolour by the American painter Thomas Birch, from the M. & M. Karolik Collection, Museum of Fine Arts, Boston, shows the Delaware River front in Philadelphia. This port city served as capital of the United States from 1790 to 1800.

New York City is seen from Long Island in this original drawing by Archibald Robertson in 1794. Most Americans still lived in rural surroundings at the turn of the century.

sanitation, overcrowding, crime and growing numbers of vagrants and paupers all became part of the American urban scene. By far the biggest danger was fire. Town houses were built close together for protection against Indian attack, and if one house went up in flames, whole blocks might be reduced to ashes in a short time. Boston had such widespread, devastating fires during its early years that the whole town was almost destroyed several times. Municipal authorities tried to ban wooden houses, but the ban could not be enforced because other building materials were too scarce and expensive.

Fire-fighting methods were primitive and rendered even less effective by a shortage of water. The techniques used in the European cities were not much better until the fire pump was introduced. As soon as the news of this invention reached American shores, Boston rushed to order one from England. It arrived three years later, in 1679, giving Boston the most up-to-date fire-fighting equipment available. Even the city of Paris did not get its first fire pump for another twenty years.

As the towns grew, problems with paupers increased. At first the busy little ports tried to keep out strangers who did not seem to have any skills or means of livelihood. But this proved impossible, and soon the growing towns were forced to adopt their own versions of the English Poor Laws rather than have people roaming about the streets homeless and hungry. The town of Newport, for example, was required by law in 1647 to "provide carefully for the relief of the poore, to maintayne the impotent, and to employ the able, and . . . appoint an overseer for the same purpose."

Such laws were adequate as long as the number of paupers remained fairly small. But during hard times the towns ran short of funds to care for all their poor. This happened repeatedly when large numbers of rural people fled to the towns for protection during Indian attacks and had no way of earning a living once they got there.

By the end of the seventeenth century, it seemed clear that pauperism was an inevitable by-product of urban growth. Boston, with a population of only about 7,000, already had a sizable class of jobless poor, while the smaller towns of Newport and New York were experiencing similar growing pains.

Epidemics, too, were another frightening aspect of urban life. Like everything else in the New World, diseases were usually imported from abroad, entering by means of the port towns. Smallpox and dysentery were two of the infectious illnesses that regularly swept through the coastal settlements. The first smallpox epidemic in Boston in 1666 claimed forty lives, while a second in 1678 killed about eight hundred people. As the young clergyman Cotton Mather wrote during the second epidemic: "Never was it such a time in Boston. Boston burying places never filled so fast. . . . To have coffins crossing each other as they have been carried in the street; To have, I know not how many corpses following each other close at their heels,—to have 38 dye in one week,—6, 7, 8 or 9 in a day."

Despite the problems and hardships of trying to create a new society in the wilderness, the young towns flourished. Within a hundred years they had turned into full-fledged commercial cities, struggling to be as polished and sophisticated as the glittering capitals of Europe.

By the end of the eighteenth century, Baltimore had replaced Newport in the list of the five leading ports, and other large urban centres were beginning to emerge in the interior of the country. But these centres, too, were located on waterways—particularly the Ohio and Mississippi rivers—for no town

could grow very large without good water transportation to facilitate trade. Even so, by 1800 America was still mostly rural. Only the five leading Atlantic ports had populations of over 10,000, and 97 per cent of the American people still lived on farms or in small towns and villages. The situation was the same in most of the other regions of the world, as the great majority of men everywhere still spent their lives tilling the soil and only a relative handful lived in cities.

Many cities along the eastern seaboard of the United States have preserved or restored some of the early townhouses that lined city streets.

CHAPTER 8

THE WALLS
CAME TUMBLING DOWN

The most remarkable thing about cities down through the ages is not that they were so different from each other but that they were so similar. From the fourth millennium BC in Mesopotamia to medieval Byzantium to the nineteenth-century AD in America, cities shared certain traits that made them "cities"—despite the vast differences in culture and customs of the people who inhabited them.

In essence, "cities" were relatively small areas that contained large masses of people living and working close together. They were compact units with clearly marked borders, punctuated by gates, archways, or some other type of entrance. They had a recognizable centre or "downtown", marked by a marketplace, forum, cathedral, temple-tower, palace, or some such focal point, with the rest of the city radiating from it in all directions.

Cities were centres of commerce, culture, entertainment, learning and government. They were arenas in which hordes of diverse people came together to exchange goods, services and ideas. New social and political movements, new artistic concepts, new styles of dress and behaviour all took root first in the cities. In every civilization on every continent, the cities acted as a catalyst for change and progress.

To share in the bustling city life, people had to live in the city itself. For centuries there was no public transportation, and no speedy private transportation either. Those who lived ten or twenty miles away from a city were as effectively cut off from everyday urban activities as if they lived one hundred miles away.

Most cities were small enough for it to take no more than an hour to walk from any part of the perimeter to a central point. Within the compact urban area, houses and businesses were squeezed together side by side, along with marketplaces, religious structures and public buildings.

Most cities were girded by walls that prevented them from sprawling out into the surrounding countryside. But cities without walls also remained small in area mainly because of the lack of speedy transportation. A city had to be small enough so that food and other necessities could be distributed throughout its entire area by such slow, clumsy vehicles as pushcarts or horse-drawn wagons. In cities where the wheel and the horse were both unknown, such as those of the Incas and Aztecs, distribution of goods was even slower.

Cities—particularly walled cities —also served as places of refuge. When danger threatened, people

For hundreds of years the Spanish Steps have been a major attraction and meeting place in Rome. In this painting by Giovanni Pannini, from the New York Metropolitan Museum of Art, Rogers Fund, 1971, one can see the Bernini fountain at the base of the steps and the Church of Trinità dei Monti at the top.

from the surrounding area would seek protection behind the city's sturdy fortifications. Enemies might lay siege to a city for years without penetrating its walls; but if they eventually did overrun it, they were apt to wipe out the entire population inside. Whole empires were won or lost depending on the ability of cities to withstand siege.

Unlike the great majority of the world's population, city people were not directly engaged in agriculture. They made their living in other ways, choosing from among the many varied occupations that grew up along with the rise of urban society.

To support these city people, the rural populations had to produce a surplus of food; it was the existence of a food surplus that had made cities possible in the first place, and the continued growth of cities was feasible only as long as farmers could produce larger and larger surpluses. It can be argued that the size and number of cities in the world has been limited by the productivity of farmers.

Industry revolutionizes cities

The Industrial Revolution changed all this. Within the space of just two centuries, the Industrial Revolution wrought more changes in the basic function and structure of cities than had occurred since the rise of Sumer thousands of years before—and the end is still nowhere in sight. In fact, the type of city that eventually emerges from the modern industrial era may not even be a "city" at all, in the historical meaning of the word, but a wholly new and unique creation.

The origins of these revolutionary changes are usually traced to Britain in the eighteenth century. At that time the country was already a highly advanced pre-industrial state.

Top and centre: *London portraits made in 1616 by Dutch engraver Cornelis Visscher show an early stone version of London Bridge and the original Saint Paul's Cathedral.* Bottom: *the doubling room of a cotton-manufacturing plant, operated almost entirely by women.*

Its mines provided coal and iron— the basis of modern industry. Coal production alone had risen from 0·2 million tons in 1560 to 10·2 million tons in 1790, owing to a combination of improved techniques for mining and demand for coal as a power source. In addition, Britain controlled a vast colonial empire and had access to great quantities of raw materials at very cheap prices. Within the country itself there was a large supply of cheap labour, made up of men who were being starved off the land as more and more acres were concentrated in the hands of a few. Such concentration resulted from the desire to raise more sheep to provide wool for the profitable cloth industry.

Britain was ripe for great changes, and by the middle of the eighteenth century they came fast and furiously. By 1770 the spinning jenny replaced the ancient spinning wheel, and between 1785 and 1787 a power loom had been devised. These and other inventions made possible the mass production of enormous quantities of cotton goods and brought about dramatic changes in the textile industry.

Earlier in the eighteenth century the British had discovered a cheaper and more efficient method of smelting iron with the use of coke—coal from which some of the gases and impurities had been removed. This was followed by the harnessing of steam-power to replace manpower as in James Watt's engine. From there it was a short hop to the successful use of the steamboat in 1807 by the American Robert Fulton, followed by the construction in Britain of the first successful steam-driven locomotive by George Stephenson in 1814. The first railroad began operating in 1825, and by 1830 two cities that had grown up with the Industrial Revolution—

Top: *smoke pours out of the chimneys of an early-nineteenth-century ironworks.* Centre: *a painting of Louis XVI distributing coins to French peasants.* Bottom: *Robert Fulton's* Clermont, *launched in 1807, was the first commercially successful steamboat in America.*

Houses and a factory stand side by side in this urban setting. Before modern methods of mass transportation were developed, people had to live close to where they worked.

Manchester and Liverpool—were linked by rail.

The lathe, the steam carriage, the steam shovel and the cotton gin were just a few other of the countless new mechanical devices that came into use. In America Eli Whitney set up a musket factory based on the principle of the division of labour. Instead of a worker making a whole musket by himself, he specialized in making just one of the parts. Other workers made other parts, and then the pieces were assembled into the final product. Such a system rested on the standardization of parts, so that each trigger or gun stock was exactly the same size as every other trigger or gun stock, making the parts interchangeable. This meant that a soldier could carry spare parts with him and repair a broken musket on the battlefield.

Whitney's system was a whole new approach to production, enabling fewer men to produce more goods more quickly than ever before. Years later, assembly lines and conveyor belts would speed up the production process to an incredible pace, but at the same time it would become monotonous and unchallenging for the worker, robbing him of pride in his craftsmanship.

Along with the new inventions and the rise of factories came the

The church steeples of Quebec, Canada, loom in the distance as people gather along the shore to watch the Royal William *begin its 1833 trans-Atlantic voyage to Gravesend, England. This was the first full steam crossing of the Atlantic.*

Boats laden with goods produced by the nineteenth-century factories of Barrow-in-Furness, Lancashire, England, sail down the southwest coast of the Furness peninsula. Industry was already polluting city air.

growth of a new type of city—the industrial city. Characterized by giant chimneys that belched black soot over the streets and tenements below, the industrial cities were dismal places to live. Many of them had once been commercial centres, but after the Industrial Revolution took hold, factory work dominated every aspect of their existence. In England and Scotland the cities of Liverpool, Birmingham, Manchester and Glasgow were among the leading industrial centres, while London prospered from the enormous volume of trade inspired by industry. All the world clamoured for Britain's manufactured goods, and Manchester alone produced more textiles than any other place on earth.

British factories and mines grew ever more greedy for cheap labour, so that women and children were pressed into service. Working and living conditions were wretched in the grime-covered factory cities. In mid-nineteenth-century Liverpool more than one half of the working-class children died before the age of five. The average life expectancy of workers was not much more than fifteen years.

Industrial cities everywhere were similar. People were crowded together within a short distance of the

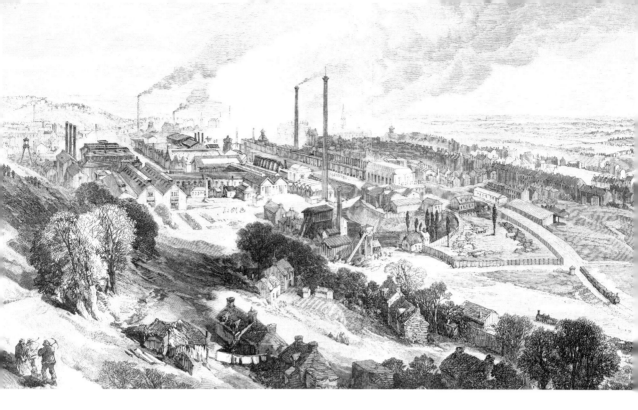

mill in which they worked, living in shacks, hovels or overcrowded tenements. In Vienna and Berlin tenements sprang up back to back. Most were five storeys high and were separated from each other at the rear by dark, narrow courtyards. The tenement that faced the street at least got some light and air, but the interior tenements got little of either.

In America completely new towns sprang up around the factories, but living conditions were as bad as in the older, congested European cities. People were worn out with work at an early age, for the mill whistle sounded at six in the morning and six at night, six days a week. The death rate was very high compared to that in non-industrial towns and cities, and disease and filth were rampant. In 1875, the mill town of Holyoke, Massachusetts, was described as follows:

Holyoke has more and worse tenements than any manufacturing town of textile fabrics in the state. . . . The sanitary arrangements are very imperfect, and in many cases there is no provision for carrying the slops from the sinks, but they are allowed to run wherever they can make their way. Portions of yards are covered with filth and green slime, and within 20 feet [6 metres], people are living in basements three feet [one metre] below the level of the yard.

In the face of such wretchedness, cities in Europe and the United States urgently sought ways to improve sanitary conditions and control the dreaded epidemics of typhoid and cholera that kept recurring in the industrial cities. After London's severe cholera epidemic in 1848, Britain created a Central Board of Health, one of the first public health systems. Paris built several hundred miles of underground sewers and halted the pollution of the Seine, while Manchester built a ninety-six-mile aqueduct to bring in pure water. In the 1870s Birmingham tore down a slum filled with shacks and shanties and replaced them with city-owned housing—an early example of a municipal slum clearance programme. In the 1890s Vienna municipalized the city's gas, water and street-car systems and also took control of orphanages and funeral parlours. The idea of urban planning was introduced in many cities, and urban parks and recreational facilities were built.

Cities grew larger and larger as people continued to pour into the urban-industrial centres, seeking any work they could find. By 1810 London had become the first European city with 1 million inhabitants since the days of Rome. (Tokyo, Peking and Hangchow had passed that mark much earlier, but they were still in the pre-industrial stage.) By 1850 London was up to 2·6 million inhabitants, and Paris, too, had passed the million mark. New York City's population reached 1 million in 1871, followed by

Berlin in 1880, and Vienna in 1885.

The populous cities were forced to spread out farther and farther, expanding beyond the walls that had once held them in. These walls served no purpose now; they were just relics of an earlier age. Among the first walls to go were those of London. Munich's walls were torn down in 1795. In 1857, Vienna destroyed its walls, and in 1861 the Berlin city wall was removed. Paris was one of the last major cities to follow this trend—its walls were not demolished until 1919.

The destruction of the walls symbolized the birth of the modern city. Bereft of their ancient girdles, the cities continued to spread out in all directions, creating transportation problems that had never been known before. People lived so far from where they worked that the cities had to come up with some means of public transportation.

As early as the seventeenth century, both London and Paris had horse-drawn coaches that were the equivalent of today's taxicabs. But these were for the well-to-do; the poor could not ride them back and forth from work every day. It was not until 1823 that Paris introduced a horse-drawn bus that was inexpensive enough for the general public. London adopted this type of bus six years later, and many other European and American cities followed its lead. The first subway or underground railway, using a steam-driven vehicle, made its debut in London in 1863. Budapest had a similar subway by 1896; Boston by 1898; Paris by 1900; Berlin by 1902; and New York by 1904. Electric-powered trolley cars also came into use during the late nineteenth and early twentieth centuries. In Belgium and the United States inter-urban trolleys provided excellent service.

This 1870 view of the Creuzot Colliery and Ironworks in Burgundy France, shows houses and shacks clustered around the factory, while giant clouds of industrial smoke hover in the air. The factory town was served by freight railroads (right foreground).

Early steam-powered engines for trolley cars helped meet the cities' need for cheap, speedy mass transportation.

Unsanitary conditions in the industrialized, heavily populated cities led to frequent outbreaks of typhoid and cholera. Here piles of garbage decay on the streets of lower Manhattan in New York City in 1895.

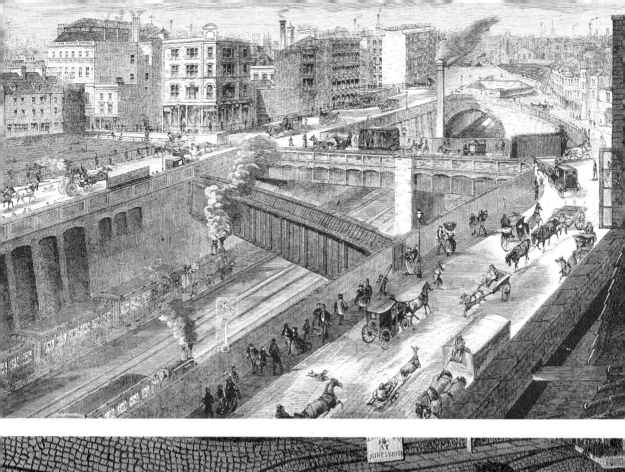

These new means of transportation had come about in response to the cities' rapid growth; but the existence of speedy transportation facilities enabled the cities to spread out still more. New neighbourhoods sprang up in an ever-widening circle around the inner core, with millions of people in the giant cities criss-crossing the streets by subway and trolley.

Agricultural products from the country were hauled into the cities by railroad or steamboat, and the growth of these two long-distance transport methods opened up regions that had been inaccessible before. In the United States, in particular, the railroad and the steamboat accelerated the development of the nation and were responsible for the creation of many new cities. Chicago—a swampy town that became the junction for ten railroad trunk lines and eleven branch lines—grew into a metropolis of over 3 million people between 1830 and 1930. Its growth was all the more remarkable considering that in 1830 it had just fifty inhabitants.

Cities and motor cars

The twentieth century also saw the birth of an invention whose impact on cities cannot yet be measured fully: the motor car. At first this was a rare and costly toy for the rich, but as the century wore on it was priced within reach of the middle and working classes. In the years following World War II, ownership of private cars multiplied by enormous leaps. The United States set the pace, with millions of workers buying their own cars at a time when these machines were still an expensive luxury in the war-torn countries of Europe. American cities became jam-packed with automobiles that clogged the streets and emitted poisonous exhaust fumes into the air, which was already being polluted by factory smoke.

The cars created new problems for the American cities, but they also provided a means by which people could escape these problems. Once a man owned his own car, he no longer had to live in the inner city and face the noise, dirt, congestion and traffic twenty-four hours a day. He could live elsewhere and drive back and forth from his city job; or he could drive to the nearest suburban railroad station and commute by train. For the first time in history, the urban working man was freed from the need to live near his job. He could live over twenty miles away, and it would still take him only about an hour to get to work—the same amount of time it had taken people in ancient Rome to walk from the perimeter of the city to the centre.

The emergence of motorized vehicles also meant that goods could be distributed more quickly and easily to areas outside the central cities. Trucks loaded with clothing, appliances, furniture and other goods could speed along the roads, unloading their merchandise in one suburban store after another. This made the central cities less necessary as marketplaces, for suburbanites could find whatever they needed in their own small but well-stocked shopping centres; they did not have to depend on the city as much any more.

In the postwar years, suburban rings grew up around the American cities, luring millions of white-collar and blue-collar workers. Once they became suburbanites, they no longer paid city taxes, thereby undermining the economic base of the cities. Farmlands and open countryside receded farther and farther from the urban centres, while neat, look-alike suburbs took their place. Although

Trains going in and out of the Farringdon Road Station of the Metropolitan Railway, London, are powered by steam engines. But on the streets above, horse-drawn carriages are still the rule.

Mass transportation in New York City before the advent of motor cars and subways. Horse-drawn buses carried passengers along the cobblestone streets. Shown here is a detail of The Third Avenue Railroad Depot, a painting by J. H. Schenck. (Metropolitan Museum of Art, Edward W. C. Arnold Collection of New York Prints, Maps, and Pictures. Bequest of Edward W. C. Arnold, 1954.)

Apartment houses overlook Lake Mälaren in this suburb of Stockholm, Sweden, called Norr Mälarstramd, which was begun in 1935. The advent of the automobile accelerated suburban growth all over the world.

people still fought for living space in such desirable and expensive cosmopolitan centres as New York, Chicago and San Francisco, many of the smaller industrial and commercial cities had trouble holding on to their middle-class populations. Everyone who could afford a car and a small house seemed to be moving to the suburbs. Generally only the poor were remaining behind in the inner cities.

In Europe, where far fewer people had cars, this trend was not yet so apparent. The number of car-owners in the major European cities in 1960 was about equal to the number of car-owners in the American cities in the 1920s, but this figure was rapidly rising. If car ownership was the single most important reason for the exodus from the inner city in the United States, then this trend should not be regarded as a uniquely American phenomenon. It means only that America had a head start in this direction, and the advanced European countries are heading this way too.

Between 1960 and 1970 the population in the central cities of the United States grew by only 1 per cent, while the suburban rings around them grew 28 per cent. The census of 1970 showed that 73·5 per cent of the American people were living in urbanized areas, which includes central cities and their suburbs. But for the first time the suburban population (76 million) exceeded both the population of the central cities (61 million) and the rural and small town populations (67 million).

If the trend continues, nearly one half of the total population of the United States will be living in the suburbs by the 1980s, while only one quarter will be living in the central cities.

Aside from the greater mobility provided by the automobile, there are other, fundamental reasons for the inner-city exodus in the United States. Cities had once been the place where people came for entertainment and for intellectual and cultural stimulation. Museums, libraries, theatres, sports tournaments, circuses, concerts and operas were all part of a city's attractions. It was here that orators and politicians could find their largest audiences, and here that writers and artists could seek each other out.

But the invention of radio and television brought large-scale entertainment for the first time right into people's homes, no matter where they lived. A man might sit in his suburban home thirty miles outside Boston, Philadelphia or Detroit and watch an excellent movie or play in his own living room. Once a family bought a television set, they did not have to live in the city to have entertainment close at hand; they did not even have to *visit* the city.

Radio and television, as well as the telephone made cities less necessary as centres for the exchange of ideas. People used to have to come together, often in an urban market-place, just to talk; but today they can use the telephone. Politicians and other public figures can com-

A bed of flowers and a memorial stone set off the tall, sleek buildings in the new industrial centre of Kharkov in the Soviet Union.

municate with millions of people at once over the airwaves, whereas in earlier times they had to speak directly to the people in some central gathering place. What the agora was to the ancient Greek, and the forum was to the early Roman, radio, television and the telephone are to the modern American.

With all these substitutes available, living in the central cities was apparently not rewarding enough or necessary enough to offset all the problems such as congestion, dirt, noise, crime and high rents that have always been a part of city life.

Today, the inner cities of the United States are declining. Even businesses, department stores, movie theatres and hotels have begun to move out. They are going to where the people are—the suburbs. Factories are relocating in pleasant, grassy industrial parks, while stores and restaurants are finding that business is better in the suburban shopping centres where there is plenty of room for customers to park.

The steady outward movement of people and businesses is creating vast new urbanized regions that have usurped many of the functions of the aging inner cities. These regions are entirely different from "cities" in that they have no precise boundaries, no single recognizable centre and, most important, no single government.

Such developments seem to be rendering the old inner cities of America obsolete, both as places to live and as cultural, intellectual and entertainment centres. Clearly their function is changing. It is conceivable that several centuries from now the cities of the United States—and possibly of some of the other advanced industrial nations—will bear no resemblance at all to the cities of old. Perhaps they will have been transformed into giant commercial or industrial parks—places inhabited by factories and skyscrapers, where millions of people work but where no one actually lives. A transition is taking place now, and what the end-product will be is still very uncertain.

But such changes are only just beginning in countries that are already highly urbanized and industrialized, with relatively high standards of living. The great majority of the world's people— three quarters of the earth's population—is nowhere near this point yet. For them, urbanization is just getting under way, and the mass movement is towards the central cities, not away from them.

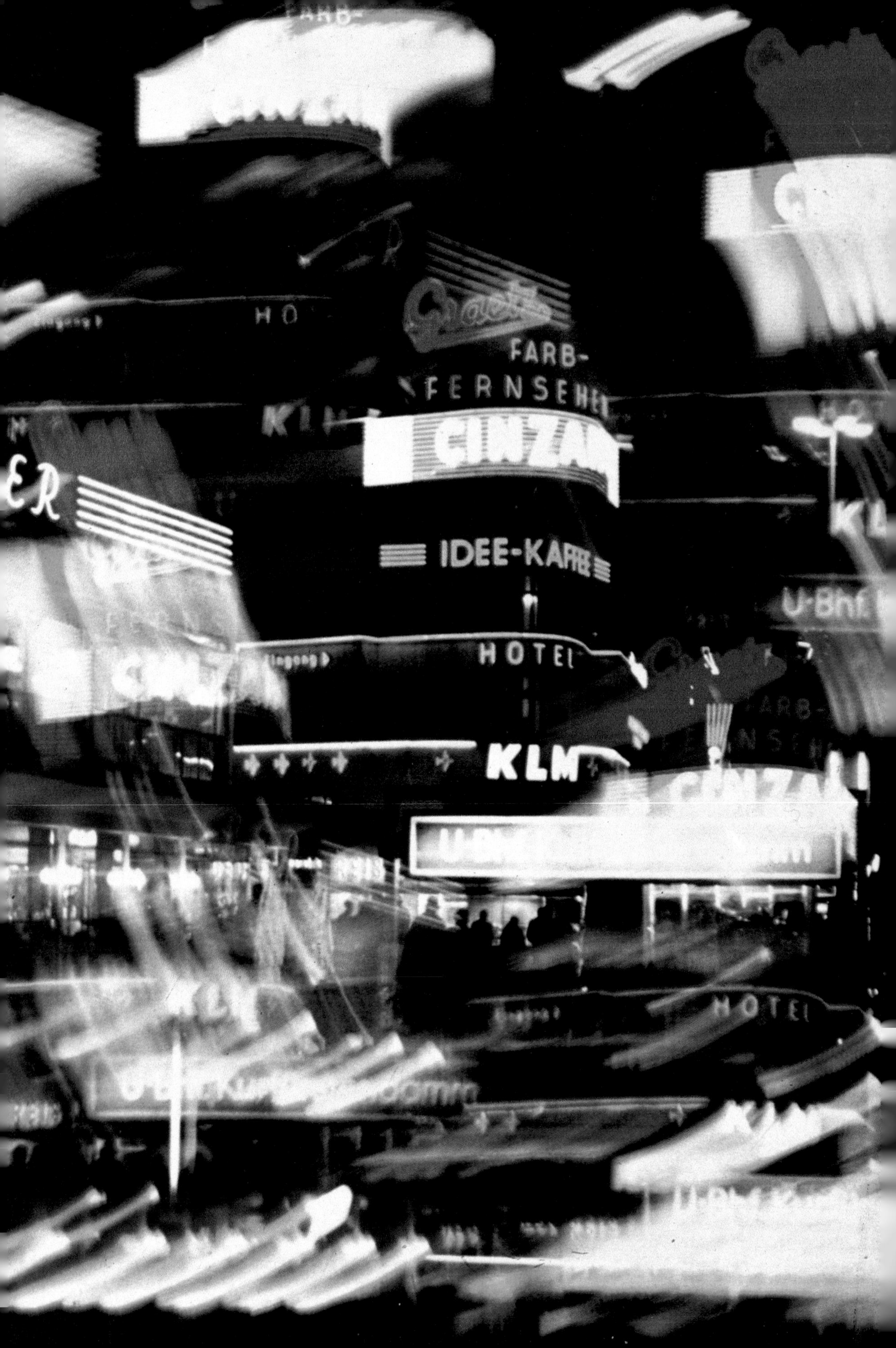
FARB-
FERNSEHEN
IDEE-KAFFEE
HOTEL
KLM

CHAPTER 9

THE WORLD
BECOMES A CITY

No matter how the city of the future is structured, one thing is clear: cities are taking over as the leading habitations of the world's people. It is estimated that by the year 2050 more than half of the world's population will live in cities of 100,000 or more.

Cities have swelled to gargantuan size. When we recall that London's population did not reach 1 million until 1810—and it was the first European city to grow so large since ancient Rome—it is startling to look at current population figures:

WORLD'S LARGEST CITIES

City	Population	Year
1 Tokyo	9,005,000	1969
2 New York	7,895,563	1970
3 London	7,703,400	1969
4 Moscow	6,942,000	1970
5 Shanghai	6,900,000	1957
6 Bombay	5,700,358	1970
7 São Paulo	5,684,706	1968
8 Cairo	4,961,000	1970
9 Rio de Janeiro	4,207,322	1968
10 Peking	4,010,000	1957
11 Seoul	3,794,959	1966
12 New Delhi	3,772,457	1970
13 Buenos Aires	3,600,000	1970
14 Leningrad	3,513,000	1970
15 Tientsin	3,320,000	1957
16 Calcutta	3,158,838	1970
17 Mexico City	3,025,564	1970
18 Osaka	3,018,000	1969

Source: United Nations Statistical Office

The figures above are for populations within the cities' boundary lines. But such statistics do not even begin to show the extent of urban development in these regions, for they do not include the suburbs and industrial areas that extend for miles and miles round the cities. These rings, together with the central cities, are known as "metropolitan areas"

A multiple-exposure photograph of a night scene in Berlin captures the feeling of excitement in large cities all over the world.

Suburban communities that extend central cities, like this development outside Los Angeles, California, are often criticized for the monotony of their design, the starkness of their treeless streets, and the lack of long-range planning that often results in the destruction of the natural landscape.

or "greater cities". But even they do not show the full urbanization picture, for, in many built-up regions, the suburban rings round one large city overlap the suburban rings round another large city many miles away. This creates vast urban-industrial stretches where little if any farmland or open countryside remains. Concrete, steel and glass are everywhere, interrupted only by small patches of suburban lawns. The growth of these regions has given rise to such words as "megalopolis" and "conurbations".

The table below shows how many people are actually living in the solid urban stretches that extend out from the city listed. These stretches may actually include several cities. For example, the urbanized area radiating from Tokyo includes the city of Yokohama (population 2,082,000 in 1965), plus neighbouring smaller cities, towns and villages. The New York urban area covers something like 2,514 square miles (6,511 square kilometres). In contrast, ancient Rome was only 5 square miles (13 square kilometres) in AD 274.

Largest urban areas

Region	Population	Year
1 New York	16,206,841	1970
2 Tokyo	14,770,727	1965
3 Paris	9,250,647	1970*
4 Mexico City	8,541,070	1970
5 Buenos Aires	8,408,930	1970
6 Los Angeles	8,351,266	1970
7 London	8,104,050	1968
8 Osaka	7,781,000	1965
9 Moscow	7,061,000	1970
10 Shanghai	6,977,000	1958

* estimate   *Source: 1972 World Almanac*

Between 1920 and 1960 the world's urban population (localities of 20,000 and more) grew from about 253 million to 753 million. Today, 25 per cent of all the people in the world live in urban areas. If, as the experts predict, the number of urban dwellers will swell to over 50 per cent in less than a century, it would be a monumental change from all past history. For even though the destiny of the world has been shaped by cities, only a small fraction of the world's population ever lived in cities before.

The vast majority of men throughout history have lived close to the land, in rural villages or tribes that were bound by age-old traditions. Life moved slowly there, and changes lagged far behind those of the fast-paced cosmopolitan centres.

Beginning in the nineteenth century, however, urbanization accelerated rapidly as a result of the Industrial Revolution. By now, more than one half of the population of North America and almost half of the population of Australia and New Zealand live in cities of at least 100,000. In South America and Europe about one third of the people live in cities of at least 100,000. Only Asia and Africa remain overwhelmingly rural, with 90 per cent of the people still living in agricultural villages and on farms. But even this picture is beginning to change.

The speed with which urbanization is now taking place stands in sharp contrast to the very gradual development of cities over thousands of years. Today's feverishly accelerated pace of urbanization, with its accompanying technological changes, has had the effect of uprooting people, destroying ancient traditions and beliefs, and breeding instability. For example, the urbanization and industrialization currently taking place in India is helping to break down the caste system that has regulated Indian life for thousands of years.

In Africa ancient tribal customs and regulations are disintegrating under the impact of urbanization. Young African tribesmen have been leaving the impoverished rural lands to seek work in the large cities. Although such migrations are often temporary and seasonal, the fact

Top: *people of the same race or religion sometimes are found within a single area, often because they are excluded from other parts of a city. One such community is "Chinatown", San Francisco, California, U.S.A.* Centre and bottom: *old and new blend in Africa, where Nigerian men in traditional garb bicycle to town on modern paved roads; where Kikuyu dancers form a striking contrast with the modern buildings in Nairobi, Kenya.*

that so many Africans are experiencing urban life—and are exposed to outside cultures and ideas—has had the effect of weakening tribal unity. In fact, many of the tribes are now divided into "modern" and "traditional" factions that are philosophically at war with one another.

When an African tribesman leaves his rural home for the city, it may be the first time in his life that he mingles freely with people of other tribes. This is especially true if his own tribe is only a minority in the city. In the following account—from an essay by Peter Gutkind, "African Urbanism, Mobility and the Social Network"—a young African relates his experiences in Mulago, an urban region just outside Kampala, the capital of Uganda. Many Africans who live in Mulago work in the government and business offices in Kampala. Others work at the large Mulago hospital, or in shops in Mulago. The majority of Africans there are from the Ganda tribe, while the remainder come from other parts of East Africa. The writer, a non-Ganda, states:

When I first arrived in Mulago I looked for any person of my tribe I knew. I was lucky to find a friend and I stayed with him for three weeks before I found a place for myself. I had a little money when I arrived but after four days in Mulago almost half of it was stolen. My friend introduced me to his friends (not all of whom were of the same tribe) to ask for jobs. Eventually I found work as a sweeper in a big office.

I now live with a group of young men only one of whom is a member of my tribe but two others work in the same office as messengers. We go to work together because one of them has a bicycle and I can ride with him. . . .

I am now trying to get better work where I can get more money. So I went to see a Ganda friend of mine. He likes me because I can speak his language.

But I do not really like the Ganda people because they treat us all with contempt.

On Sunday I play football. I have joined a club and pay one shilling every three months. There are people from many different tribes in my club but we get on well together. I sometimes get tired of living here and having to buy all my food. If I get tired of work I go home, but I always come back.

East Africa is the least urbanized part of that continent, with only 2·7 per cent of the population living in urban regions. In contrast, southern Africa (excluding Angola) is 26 per cent urban, while the Union of South Africa alone is 40 per cent urbanized.

Tribal society in Africa south of the Sahara, with its lack of commerce, did not encourage the growth of towns and cities. But once the Europeans began colonizing the continent—and particularly after gold, diamonds, coal and copper were discovered there in the second half of the nineteenth century—towns and cities began to sprout. Within ten years of the discovery of gold Johannesburg, South Africa, had a population of 100,000. Capetown, Kimberley and Durban also grew into large cities, and by 1890 there were more than two thousand miles of rail tracks stretching across southern Africa. Zambia and southern Rhodesia also developed along industrial and commercial lines, with mining a primary industry. Today about 25 per cent of the population of these two countries live in cities.

The pattern of urban-industrial development in southern Africa is not typical of what has been happening in other parts of Africa, or in the underdeveloped countries of Asia and Latin America. There, cities are growing to enormous sizes, but their growth has not been accompanied

by a really substantial growth of industry. Nor are their rural populations declining. Although these countries are urbanizing too, it is quite different from the way it occurred in Europe and the United States between the eighteenth and early twentieth centuries.

Urbanization in the advanced countries was mainly the product of industrialization. In the United States, in particular, people left their small, unproductive farms because they could make a better living in the cities. Factories, mines, railroads and commercial businesses beckoned to them, offering them greater opportunities than they could hope to find on the land. As large numbers of people left the rural areas, farms became consolidated in the hands of fewer and fewer people.

While modernization is coming to India, many of the old ways are still maintained. The throngs of people here are attending a religious festival at the New Delhi Great Mosque.

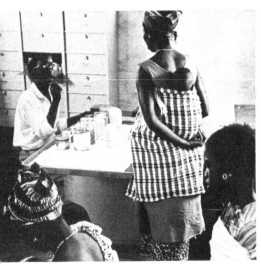

Agriculture was also affected by the Industrial Revolution, and new, more efficient farming methods were introduced. The mechanical seeder, the reaper and the steam-powered thresher were just a few of the nineteenth-century farming inventions that increased the yield of the land. By the mid-twentieth century, powerful "combines" were zipping across huge commercial farms, reaping and threshing as they went.

Such mechanization meant that far fewer people were needed on the land because machines could do the work of many. This prompted still more people to leave the farms for the greater promise of the cities. In the United States today, only 5 per cent of the people actually live and work on farms—and this 5 per cent produces far more food than the country needs. In fact, the government has to pay farmers *not* to grow so much. In most other industrial countries, the number of people engaged in agriculture is below 15 per cent, and still falling. In France, about 20 per cent of the people were still on farms in the early 1960s—a high percentage for an industrial nation today.

In all of these countries, advances in agriculture and industry were the main reasons for the rapid growth of the cities after 1800. But this is not what is happening in the under-developed countries today. Although the cities in Asia and Latin America are growing at a phenomenal rate—even faster than the cities of the industrial nations were growing in their heyday—this growth has been due mainly to a high birth rate, not to industrialization. There have also been advances in medicine and health care that have lowered the death rate, creating a large excess of births over deaths and swelling the urban populations to the bursting point.

In Ceylon, for example, the death rate dropped by 34 per cent between 1946 and 1947, as a result of spraying with DDT, which reduced the incidence of malaria. Such a sharp decline in the death rate did not occur in the Western countries until after they had already marched a long way towards industrialization.

Many of the largest cities in the less developed countries, such as Bombay, Calcutta, Buenos Aires and Rio de Janeiro, do not yet have enough industry and jobs to support their enormous populations. The population growth in these cities has far outpaced the growth of industry and business, and the cities themselves remain underdeveloped.

Despite this, people from the rural areas continue to migrate to the already swollen urban centres. This is because the poverty in the rural areas is even worse than in the cities. Rural populations have also been growing steadily, so that in many overcrowded farming regions the peasants can barely keep themselves alive from the yield of their meagre plots. Agriculture has not become mechanized. It has remained backward and inefficient, and there are just too many people on too little cultivated land. The rural surplus is spilling over into the cities simply because there is no other place for it to go.

But all too often when the migrants get to the cities they cannot find work. In almost every large city in the underdeveloped world, decrepit slums of "junk houses" have sprung up on the urban fringes or in vacant lots and parks within the city itself. Unlike traditional urban slums, these wretched hovels are occupied by squatters—usually migrants from the rural areas—who can afford no rent at all. They build houses out of flattened tin cans, corrugated cardboard, or any other kind of scrap material they can get their hands on.

In such diverse cities as Caracas, Venezuela; Amman, Jordan; Bogotà, Colombia; Baghdad, Iraq; São Paulo, Brazil, and elsewhere the growth picture is very much the same. The cities have expanded tremendously over the last decade or two, but a large part of the growth has been in the slums. Gleaming modern skyscrapers of steel and concrete stand in startling contrast to the shanty towns and shacks

A city's people need entertainment, as shown in this Brazilian carnival scene.

Left: the residents of a city are provided with medical care and information. Right: a slum on the outskirts of Santiago, Chile. It is but one example of the miserable conditions under which people still live, both in and around the major cities of the world.

A market street scene in Cairo, Egypt.

The extreme crush of rush hour on city streets is a universal problem with no immediate solution in sight.

spread out nearby, and poverty is everywhere.

It is estimated that slum dwellers and squatters account for up to one half the population of the larger cities in underdeveloped countries. The squatter settlements are particularly badly off. They have grown so quickly that most cities are unable to supply them with water, sewerage, light, police protection, health centres and other normal municipal services. Usually there are not even any schools for the squatters' children to attend, and the settlements are fertile breeding grounds for crime, vice, violence and disease. Migrants coming into these settlements have little chance of rising out of their abject poverty. According to one study, 90 per cent of the migrants into Santiago, Chile, remain as poor as they were when they first entered the city; only 10 per cent are able to improve their lives at all by leaving the rural areas.

If the current growth rates continue, huge, poverty-ridden cities like Bombay are expected to have between 36 and 66 million inhabitants by the year 2000. What is more, the cities of the underdeveloped areas are not alone in their high growth rates. If the New York urban area continues to grow at the same pace, it will reach 21 million people by 1985 and 30 million by 2010. (As of 1970, it had 16,206,841 people.)

Perhaps the economies of the advanced industrial countries can keep pace with such phenomenal growth without suffering a sharp decline in their standards of living. But the underdeveloped countries can barely feed their people now. They have to industrialize and increase production as fast as they can, just to stand still; otherwise their resources will be overwhelmed by the population explosion.

Cities must find ways to make life enjoyable for urban residents and preserve humanity. Here Central Park in New York City provides some open space and trees.

Most of the countries that succeeded in industrializing started early, when their populations were still small compared to today. In the Soviet Union the major industrial push did not come until after World War I, but the country already had a sizable industrial and commercial base after the first decade of the twentieth century.

Japan is another latecomer that managed to leap ahead of its population growth and become an urban-industrial giant. However, Japan underwent cultural and social upheavals in the process of modernizing. Attitudes changed drastically, and the Japanese people began thinking in terms of keeping their family size down. By the time abortion was legalized, the Japanese people were psychologically ready for it, and it became a very effective method of population control. The birth rate in Japan has dropped sharply since World War II, and the population has been stabilizing. Today there are fewer people in the rural areas, and the majority of Japanese live in cities and work in an industrial economy.

The last frontier

In Asia, Africa and Latin America, more people are becoming urbanized every day. We are heading towards an urban world, and no place on earth is being left untouched.

In the early 1970s work was begun on a 3,000-mile road that will open up the largest unexplored region still left—Brazil's Amazon jungle. The Trans-Amazon Highway will cut right through the heart of the jungle where no civilized man has ever set foot before. The road is expected to open up an area half as big as the United States for settlement and exploitation.

The effects of the road-building work can be seen already in the drowsy little river towns that dot the more accessible parts of the jungle. The population of the town of Altamira doubled in 1971, jumping from 3,000 to 6,000 inhabitants. Centrally generated electric power was installed for the first time, and new houses, bars and brothels have sprung up. Road-building crews pile into the town on weekends, turning Altamira into a boisterous, free-wheeling boom town.

This is the new frontier now, and also one of the last frontiers. Within five years the Brazilian government expects at least 500,000 landless peasants from the poverty-stricken northeast to settle along the new highway. Large towns and then cities will surely follow, as the inevitable process of urbanization gets under way.

CHAPTER 10

PLANNED CITIES

As the world hurtles towards urbanization, nations are delving into the problem of how to harness and control the urban octopus; how to eliminate the worst aspects of city living and keep the best; and how to create the ideal city. It may be beyond their power to halt the frenzied urban growth that was touched off two centuries ago by the Industrial Revolution, but they can try to make the best of the inevitable by careful planning.

In the past, most cities were not planned; they just "happened": that is, they grew up spontaneously, with no grand design worked out for them in advance. Usually they were the natural outgrowth of villages and towns that happened to prosper. Rome started out as a small village, as did Athens, Paris, London and New York. Of course, there were exceptions to this general rule. In ancient times, Alexander the Great planned and built seventy new cities, the most successful of which was Alexandria in Egypt, which had nearly 1 million inhabitants at its ancient peak of population. Czar Peter the Great of Russia used hundreds of thousands of convicts, peasants and prisoners-of-war to build his capital city of Saint Petersburg, now Leningrad. The capital of the United States, Washington, D.C., was also a planned city. But

This starkly modernistic building is part of the Indian city of Chandigarh. Built mainly in the 1950s, Chandigarh represents a modern attempt to create the ideal city.

for the most part, cities throughout history were not the products of deliberate thought.

Today the reverse is true. Many nations, alarmed by the urban sprawl that has been gobbling up farmland and open countryside, and appalled by the congestion, traffic, slums and pollution in the central cities, have begun building new cities that are specifically designed to meet modern needs. Futuristic concepts such as Britain's "Sea City" may seem too far-fetched for these nations to consider at the moment, but as more of the world becomes overpopulated, they may well follow Britain's lead in planning such urban experiments.

Britain has long been a pioneer in planning new cities. As the first nation to become industrialized and urbanized, it faced staggering urban problems long before anyone else. In 1898 an Englishman, Sir Ebenezer Howard, published a book called *To-morrow: a Peaceful Path to Real Reform*, in which he advocated a new form of urban growth and organization: the "garden city". Such a city combined the beauty of nature—trees, grass, sunshine and fresh air—with all the advantages of city living, including an abundance of jobs, social and cultural centres and good shopping facilities. The garden city was to be fairly small in size and surrounded by green belts, so that the inhabitants would have easy access to the countryside, while at the same time they would be close to their work. The green belts would also serve as a "wall", preventing the new city from spreading out too far.

In 1899 Howard organized the Garden City Association and in 1903 built the first garden city, Letchworth. It was not a very great success, but Howard still had enough faith in his idea to try again. In 1920 he started building a second demonstration model, Welwyn Garden City, which was only twenty miles northwest of London. This project, too, encountered many difficulties and failed to arouse widespread enthusiasm. Nevertheless, both Welwyn and Letchworth survived and grew, and in later years—particularly after World War II—British planners looked at them with renewed interest.

The war had given the British a painful lesson in the weakness of modern, heavily populated cities. Cities were not the places of refuge they had once been. On the contrary, the invention of the aeroplane had made them the most vulnerable targets for attack. Aerial warfare made it clear that people were far safer outside the great urban centres. It was better not to concentrate so much of the population and industrial resources in a few large cities, but to spread them out into many smaller towns and cities. Fast, modern transportation methods made such dispersal possible. Furthermore, these new towns—modelled on Howard's garden cities—could also drain off the surplus population of the large cities, reliev-

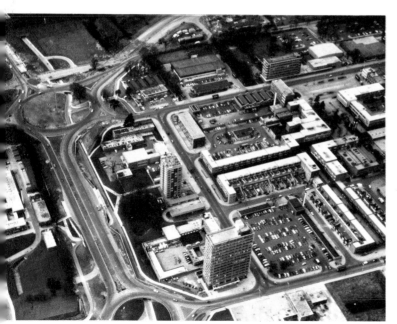

Aerial photo shows the row, or terrace, houses, high-rise buildings and parking lots of Stevenage, the first of the British New Towns, which was begun in 1947.

Two-storey row houses in Stevenage, Hertford-shire, England, look out over a pedestrian walk-way. Architects planned the town so that pedes-trians would be completely separated from vehicles.

ing the overcrowded conditions, housing shortages, slums and traffic jams that plagued them.

Decentralization seemed to be the answer to many urban problems, and since many British cities had to be rebuilt after the war anyhow, it was an appropriate time to experiment with urban planning. In August, 1946, Britain passed the New Towns Act, thus becoming the first nation to set up an official programme for building new urban centres. In December, 1947, the first new town—Stevenage—was legally designated, and over the next twenty-five years at least thirty more new towns were begun.

Eight of the towns were built in a ring round London, separated from the city by a green belt about five miles wide that was reserved for agriculture, recreation and other rural uses. Thus the physical spread of London's suburbs was halted, for the time being.

Most of the new towns that have gone up so far are designed for populations of about 35,000 to 60,000, and each has its own industrial region that should provide jobs for the majority of residents. Each town also has a main centre for shopping, theatres, pubs, restaurants and offices, surrounded by several residential neighbourhoods that contain their own primary schools, marketing areas and playing fields. Most of the dwellings are one- or two-storey row houses, with a few three-storey buildings, all of which have fenced gardens. The industrial regions are set off from the residential neighbourhoods so that they do not interfere with the rustic setting of trees, lawns and gardens.

The main purpose of the towns round London was to relieve the congestion of the metropolis. New towns elsewhere in England, Scotland and Wales had other purposes. For example, the towns of Peterlee and Glenrothes were set up as urban replacements for several nondescript mining villages in the area. The town of Corby was built to handle a population spurt stemming from the expansion of a steel complex, and East Kilbride and Cumbernauld were meant as homes for Glasgow's overflowing population.

Although the British new towns have been highly successful so far, they have had their share of problems. In the early years, many of the working-class families that had been

Model shows a residential section of the British new town of Milton Keynes. Cars are restricted to the fringes of the housing section.

The noted German architect Walter Gropius, one of the leaders of the modern "functional" school of architecture, designed this new town near Berlin. Traffic flows round the high-rise buildings in a circular pattern.

relocated in the new towns were lonely and unhappy in their country-like surroundings. They missed the crowded, lively streets of their old city neighbourhoods and felt isolated in their garden-enclosed homes. They made many trips back to their old homes and sometimes—in spite of the more luxurious housing in the new towns—moved back to where they had come from.

Such difficulties led to some changes in design. For example, the towns of Cumbernauld and Glenrothes dropped the idea of individual gardens, replacing them with larger open spaces for community use. The developers also began building more housing units per acre, giving the towns more of the urban atmosphere with which the residents were familiar.

Some of the newer communities have been designed on a larger scale to begin with. The town of Washington, near Newcastle-upon-Tyne, has been building about 1,000 new houses a year to keep up with a labour force that has been growing by some 5,000 a year. By the end of the century the city is expected to have a population of 100,000. The city of Milton Keynes, located near Northampton about seventy miles from London, will be even larger—it is expected to house about 250,000 people.

France, Belgium, Italy, West Germany and the Netherlands have also been building new towns and industrial parks since the end of World War II. With so many of their cities and resources destroyed by bombs, these countries have undergone reconstruction on a large-scale basis. Cities that had existed since the Middle Ages were rebuilt to cope with modern traffic and housing needs, while industry was encouraged to build new plants away from the large urban centres.

In the Netherlands, for example, industrial parks have been set up in areas of high unemployment, such as Limburg province in the southeast where coal mining is petering out. To induce firms to move into these industrial parks, the government has been paying half the land costs.

Another nation that has been heavily involved in building new towns and cities is Israel, although the motivation is quite different. At the time that Israel proclaimed its independence in 1948, about 60 per cent of its territory was a desert wasteland. But Israel was determined to make use of whatever land it had, and by now the country has reclaimed 65 per cent of its desert by irrigation.

One of the new desert towns— Arad—is expected to house about 60,000 people once it is fully developed. But actually the town is not new. Another town was built on the same site about five thousand years ago by the Canaanites, who were also able to work wonders with irrigation. Afterwards, eleven other towns rose and fell in the same area, and their remains are still buried in the giant mound of sand and rubble called Tell Arad.

Before deciding whether it is feasible to build a town in the desert, Israeli engineers have to make a survey, stake out the area and see if they can start some small-scale farming. While doing this preliminary work, they live in tents. Afterwards they build temporary asbestos houses for themselves and set up shops, clinics, a community room, a library, a post office and other small municipal services.

In the second stage of construction, the workers build more temporary housing, set up the facilities for full-scale construction and begin working on the permanent installa-tions. This job may take about five years, and while it is still going on, the people and industry begin moving in.

The town of Arad consists of six housing clusters, each containing 5,000 dwelling units. It is a highly experimental town where new concepts in layout and traffic patterns are being tested. For example, parking is permitted only on the outside of each housing cluster, on the periphery of the residential areas. No cars are allowed inside at all; only pedestrian traffic is permitted. There are no streets to cross, and children do not have to dodge cars while playing outdoors or going to school. Most of the people live in modern apartment buildings, but there is also a villa area for private luxury houses. Two resort hotels with recreation facilities and a sanitorium are among the other features of this new desert town.

The United States has also been building new towns for the last decade or so. The National Commission on Population Growth recommended the construction of 110 new towns and cities to accommodate the 100 million new United States citizens predicted by the year 2000.

The desert hills surround this new housing complex in Elath, Israel. The country has reclaimed about 65 per cent of its desert region through irrigation and is building new towns in the desert.

The new town of Reston, Virginia, outside Washington, D.C., contains a residential centre, a shopping centre (shown here), and an industrial centre to serve its residents.

Unlike Britain or Israel, the United States has been building its new towns on a private basis. Private developers have been buying up large tracts of land, usually with the backing of such corporations as Humble Oil, Westinghouse, Gulf, Goodyear, Alcoa, U.S. Steel, and Kaiser.

Among the best-known of these new towns is Columbia, Maryland, which is similar in many ways to the British new towns. Located halfway between Washington, D.C., and Baltimore, Maryland, Columbia now has about 20,000 residents and is eventually expected to house about 110,000 people. In addition to the forty-four industries that have already moved there, new plants are going up that will provide thousands of additional jobs. In time the town is expected to have plants that employ about one half its residents, with the rest commuting to work in Washington or Baltimore.

Columbia is divided into seven villages or neighbourhoods, each limited to 15,000 residents, and each clustered round a grade school, day-care centre and swimming pool. In each village there are also small grocery stores, beauty parlours, shoe-repair shops, TV repair centres and other small neighbourhood service shops. The main downtown area, which serves all the neighbourhoods, contains office buildings, a shopping mall, restaurants and theatres.

Housing in Columbia is a mixture of private homes, town houses, apartment buildings and low-income houses. Although the town may look like a typical suburb at first glance, the existence of industry, subsidized low-income housing and apartments makes it far different from most American suburbs. Also, unlike most other American suburbs, it is racially integrated. Almost 20 per cent of Columbia's residents are black, while nationally the proportion of blacks in suburbs is less than 5 per cent.

The fact that Columbia promises to be a huge financial success for its developer, James W. Rouse, indicates that it will probably be used as a model by many other private builders. Certainly it has proved to be more successful than another new town, Reston, Virginia, located eighteen miles west of Washington, D.C.

Occupying 7,400 acres, Reston was set up by a subsidiary of the Gulf Oil Company. It was an expensive town, with homes priced at $35,000 (£15,000) and more. Moreover, the architecture was so off-beat and experimental that people either loved it or hated it. Because the new town had such narrow appeal, sales and rentals lagged, bringing on a financial crisis. Finally Gulf Oil took over the development job and built a large number of more conventional homes at modest prices, thereby hoping to attract a broader range of people.

Perhaps the most ambitious example of city building in the twentieth century has been the construction of Brazil's new capital, Brasília. The purpose of this project was not only to build a gleaming,

modern national capital city, but to open up the heartland of Brazil.

Most of Brazil's population is crowded into the coastal regions, while the jungle-covered interior has remained practically unsettled. As far back as 1789 there was talk of building an interior capital, but at that time there was no way to transport heavy construction equipment so far inland.

Modern technology finally made the idea of an inland capital feasible, and in April, 1960, work was begun on the new city of Brasília. Thousands of construction workers and much equipment were flown 600 miles from the coast into the interior of Brazil to begin building a city in the middle of nowhere. Its only link to the outside world was an airport, although the government planned eventually to connect it with all parts of Brazil via thousands of miles of new highway. (The Trans-Amazon Highway, begun in the early 1970s, is part of this network.)

Set atop a lofty, dry plateau, Brasília posed innumerable problems for the construction crews. From time to time, the electric power failed; there were perpetual shortages of food and water; and there were many exasperating delays in getting supplies.

Nevertheless, the city that was taking shape in the wilderness was a spectacular sight. Tall glass buildings jutted up into the sky, towering over the artificial lakes that reflected the rays of the sun. Miles and miles of roads curved in and around the city, and an assortment of oddly shaped structures made it seem like a "world of tomorrow". The government secretariat building resembled two tall dominoes standing next to each other, connected in the middle by a bridge. One of the houses of Congress was shaped like a dome, while the other house looked like a saucer. All together, the official

Looking like a pair of giant dominoes, the government secretariat building in Brasília stands between the dome-and-saucer-shaped buildings that comprise the two houses of Congress.

A spectacular fountain, illuminated at night, draws attention to the office of the Brazilian Consulate General in the country's new capital, Brasília.

buildings and residences were said to have cost about $600 million (£250 million).

The city also featured "super blocks" of houses, stores, schools and hospitals, and a new type of traffic system that eliminated traffic lights and road crossings. Garbage disposals are invisible.

Within three years after construction started, Brasília was ready for its first occupants. The only trouble was that nobody wanted to live there. The city was just too isolated, hot and dusty. The gleaming glass buildings that looked so cool from the outside were sweltering inside—the builders had forgotten to put in air-conditioning.

But gradually people were induced to move to the new city. Once the government buildings were finished, the Brazilian President took up residence there, and most government functions were carried on from the new capital. Soon afterwards the foreign embassies moved in, and by 1967 Brasília had a population of about 300,000. The number of inhabitants is expected to reach 500,000 by 1985.

Brasília is not the only new city that has had trouble attracting residents. At the beginning of the twentieth century the Australians started building Canberra as their new capital. After they had finally

finished it in 1927, they could hardly get anyone to move into it: it was a spacious but sterile city. Far fewer people live there today than the number for which it was planned.

Chandigarh, the Indian city designed by the Swiss architect Le Corbusier in the 1940s and completed in the 1950s, has not become very popular yet because people there feel it is not Indian in character. Furthermore, certain features have turned out to be very irritating. Le Corbusier designed the homes with air holes in the outside walls to provide cross-ventilation. He apparently did not realize that the air holes would permit people in the street to overhear conversations inside the buildings. Residents who prefer privacy to cross-ventilation have plugged up the air holes.

The future—when new cities confront old problems

It is far too early yet to tell whether the new cities and towns—those that were specifically built to meet twentieth-century needs—will succeed or fail. From the British new towns to the Israeli desert cities, all of the planned urban centres are still fresh and shining. Since they only came into being after World War II, the houses are still up-to-date; there is no overcrowding yet, and no slums.

The new towns were started according to well-laid-out plans, but it remains to be seen how they will fare as succeeding generations of residents grow up, seek work, open businesses, get married and have children of their own. It is easier to start a new town than to predict and control its natural growth over a long period of time.

If a new town or city ages badly—if it becomes overcrowded and the houses deteriorate, schools decline and slums appear—many residents may move elsewhere and commute to their jobs in the city's industrial section. Then the city would be spawning its own suburbs; it would be aggravating the problem of urban sprawl instead of helping to eliminate it.

Such unpredictable factors as population growth, economic recessions, inflationary spirals, social conditions, and obsolescence or depletion of resources defy exact urban planning. In addition, even the most carefully designed plans may be out of date by the time they are fully in operation. The British town planners, for example, did not anticipate the large numbers of families who would buy their own cars, and they did not provide nearly enough garage space. Many of the new towns in the United States —built in the 1960s—have found that their garbage disposal and sewage treatment systems are not in line with the new ecological guidelines. Pollution of the environment was not a major national concern at that time, and the urban planners failed to take such matters into account.

Although the new towns and cities were designed to fill specific needs and overcome specific problems, there is no telling how they will evolve over the years. They may turn out to be very similar to the older, unplanned cities, replete with all the ills that have plagued cities throughout history; or they may grow up untroubled by many of the old urban problems, only to find themselves facing new and different problems that are equally hard to solve.

Factories in this recently constructed industrial park in Germany are already somewhat outdated because they lack anti-pollution devices.

ACKNOWLEDGMENTS

Cover by Akira Sakaguchi. Endpapers courtesy of Japan Air Lines. Air India: pp. 15 (top), 108, 116, 124. APA: S. Ipolito, p. 85; Prenzel, p. 71 (bottom). Arab Information Center: p. 39 (bottom). Archaeological Institute of America: American School of Classical Studies in Athens, p. 46; J. Walter Graham, p. 42; Jericho Excavation Fund, p. 29; R. V. Schoder, pp. 87, 88; Phoebe A. Sheftel, p. 48 (bottom); Saul S. Weinberg, pp. 16, 40, 41, 43 (top). Brazilian Consulate-General: pp. 112 (top), 123 (bottom). British Information Services: pp. 8, 12–13 (top centre), 118, 119, 120 (top). British Museum: pp. 18, 21 (top, first from top, bottom), 22, 23, 24, 26 (top), 27 (top), 34, 35 (top left and right, centre), 37 (bottom), 96 (top and centre). British Tourist Office: p. 72. Chicago Convention and Tourism Bureau: p. 10. Decco Doi: pp. 14 (top), 115. Deutsches Museum: p. 80 (left). Egyptian Tourist Office: p. 12 (left centre). FPG: pp. 60, 75, 112 (bottom right); Bernhart, p. 58; Gerald Clyde, p. 64; Edwards, p. 61 (top); William Gelman, p. 84; Gridley, p. 114 (bottom); Konarak-M. Epp, p. 111; McCoy, p. 93; Ellis Sawyer, p. 107; Bernard Silverstein, p. 63 (top), Ulf Sjostedt, p. 65; Stark Studios, p. 109 (top); Tremaine, p. 109 (centre). French Government Tourist Office: pp. 2, 4 (top), 66, 69, 71 (centre right). German Information Center: pp. 4 (both centre photos), 12 (centre right), 14 (lower left), 15 (bottom), 67, 106, 120 (bottom), 125.

Greek National Tourist Office: pp. 47, 48 (top), 49 (bottom), 50. Gulf Reston Inc.: Linda Bartlett, p. 112. Israeli Government Tourist Office: pp. 12 (bottom right), 14 (lower right), 121. Italian Cultural Institute: pp. 53, 54, 55 (bottom), 56, 57. Italian Government Travel Office: pp. 55 (top), 80 (right). Japan National Tourist Office: p. 13 (top right). William Loren Katz: pp. 59, 89, 97 (centre). KLM Aerocarto: p. 9 (top and centre). The Mansell Collection: pp. 17, 19 (top), 21 (second from top), 25, 28, 30, 32, 33, 36, 37 (top), 38, 39 (top), 43 (bottom), 44, 45, 49 (top), 70, 81, 96 (bottom), 97 (top and bottom), 98, 99, 100 (top and centre), 102 (top). Metropolitan Museum of Art: Edward W. C. Arnold Collection, p. 102 (bottom); Gift of John D. Rockefeller, Jr., p. 35 (bottom); Rogers Funds, p. 94. Mexican National Tourist Council: pp. 12 (top left), 82, 83. Museum of the City of New York: p. 91 (top); J. Clarence Davies Collection, p. 90; Jacob A. Riis Collection, p. 100 (bottom). Museum of Fine Arts, Boston, Massachusetts: M. Karolik Collection, p. 91 (bottom). Museum of Fine Arts, Kansas City, Missouri: William Rockhill Nelson Gallery of Fine Arts, p. 31. New York Convention and Visitors Bureau: p. 4 (bottom). New York Public Library: pp. 71 (top), 77 (top), 78. Chuck Peterson, Naval Undersea Research and Development Center, Hawaii Laboratory: p. 6. The Port Authority of New York and New Jersey: p. 11. Romanian National Tourist Office: p. 12 (bottom left). Scala New York/ Florence: pp. 73, 77 (bottom), 79; Dio, p. 105. John D. Schiff of Columbia University: p. 92. Carole Sims: p. 114 (top). Standard Oil Company: p. 9 (bottom). Swedish Tourist Traffic Association: p. 104. Turkish Information Service: pp. 61 (bottom), 62, 63 (bottom). United Nations: pp. 109 (bottom), 112 (bottom left). University Museum; University of Pennsylvania: pp. 19 (bottom), 26 (bottom), 27 (bottom). Varig Airlines: p. 123 (top).

FURTHER READING

Bell, Rose and Bell, Colin. 1969. *City Fathers: Early History of Town Planning in Britain*. Barrie & Jenkins, London.

Bridenbaugh, Carl. 1966. *Cities in the Wilderness: the first century of urban life in America, 1626–1742*. Alfred A. Knopf, New York, reprint Oxford University Press, 1971, pa.

Chamberlin, Eric R. 1966. *Everyday Life in Renaissance Times*. G. P. Putnam's Sons, New York; Batsford, London, 1966.

Crosby, Theo. 1965. *Architecture: City Sense*. Studio Vista, London.

Eells, Richard, and Walton, Clarence, eds. 1968. *Man in the City of the Future*. Collier-Macmillan Ltd, London.

Fairbrother, Nan. 1970. *New Lives, New Landscapes*. The Architectural Press, London; Penguin Books, 1972.

Fortune Magazine Editors. 1968. *The Negro and the City*. Time Inc., New York.

Fremantle, Anne. 1970. *Age of Faith* (Great Ages of Man series). Time Inc., New York; Time-Life International, Amsterdam, 1967.

Hale, John R. 1966. *Renaissance* (Great Ages of Man series). Time Inc., New York; Time-Life International, Amsterdam, 1967.

Hall, Peter. 1971. *London 2000*. Faber & Faber, London.

Hall, Peter. 1966. *World Cities*. Weidenfeld and Nicolson, London.

Higbee, Edward. 1962. *Squeeze: Cities Without Space*. Apollo, New York.

Jacobs, Jane. 1961. *The Death and Life of Great American Cities*. Random House, New York; Jonathan Cape, London, 1962.

Kramer, Samuel Noah. 1967. *Cradle of Civilization* (Great Ages of Man series). Time Inc., New York; Time-Life International, Amsterdam, 1969.

Mumford, Lewis. 1968. *The City in History: Its origins, its transformation and its prospect*. Harcourt, Brace & World, New York; Secker and Warburg, London, 1961; Penguin Books, 1966.

Nairn, Ian. 1967. *Britain's Changing Towns*. B.B.C., London.

Prescott, William H. 1966. *The History of the Conquest of Mexico*. The University of Chicago Press, Chicago; Everyman, London, 1969. (Original publication in three volumes by Harper and Brothers, 1843.) Abridged edition available.

Rodwin, Lloyd. 1956. *The British New Towns Policy: Problems and Implications*. Harvard University Press, Cambridge, Mass.

Rowling, Marjorie. 1968. *Everyday Life in Medieval Times*. G. P. Putnam's Sons, New York; Batsford, London, 1969.

Saggs, H. W. J. 1965. *Everyday Life in Babylonia and Assyria*. G. P. Putnam's Sons, New York; Batsford, London, 1965.

Schneider, Wolf. 1963. *Babylon is Everywhere*. McGraw-Hill, London.

Smailes, A. E. 1960. *The Geography of Towns*. Hutchinson, London.

INDEX